I SEE YOUR
DREAM JOB

I SEE YOUR DREAM JOB

*A Career Intuitive Shows You How to
Discover What You Were
Put on Earth to Do*

SUE FREDERICK

 ST. MARTIN'S GRIFFIN 🐦 NEW YORK

I SEE YOUR DREAM JOB. Copyright © 2009 by Sue Frederick. All rights reserved.
Printed in the United States of America. For information, address St. Martin's
Press, 175 Fifth Avenue, New York, N.Y. 10010.

www.stmartins.com

Book design by Ellen Cipriano

The Library of Congress has cataloged the hardcover edition as follows:

Frederick, Sue, 1951–
    I see your dream job : a career intuitive shows you how to discover what
you were put on earth to do / Sue Frederick. — 1st ed.
        p. cm.
    ISBN 978-0-312-55420-0
    1. Astrology. 2. Occupations—Miscellanea. 3. Vocational guidance—
Miscellanea. I. Title.
    BF1729.O25F74 2009
    131—dc22

                                                          2009016206

ISBN 978-0-312-55421-7 (trade paperback)

First St. Martin's Griffin Edition: September 2010

10   9   8   7   6   5   4   3   2   1

This book is dedicated to Paul, Crissie, Marv, my Dad, and
all the departed loved ones who at their moment of
crossing illuminated the truth behind the illusion,
and then came back in my dreams to
make sure I got it right.

CONTENTS

PART 2: FINDING YOUR INTENDED CAREER PATH / 45

PART 3: USING YOUR LIFE FUEL / 141

PART 4: TAPPING INTO YOUR OWN INTUITIVE CAREER GUIDANCE / 161

ACKNOWLEDGMENTS

I would like to thank the following people for their support in this work. I can't imagine my life without them.

To Gene, my husband, who "gets me" better than anyone ever has. Thank you for the way you held our family and home together as I spent long hours and weekends on this project. You give my life possibility, meaning, love, and best of all—laughter and fun.

Jennifer Enderlin, my editor at St. Martin's Press, thank you for your unswerving enthusiasm for this project. Your belief in me has been profoundly reassuring. Lisa Hagan, my divine book agent, your guidance, friendship, and knowledge is miraculous and such a blessing.

My friends: Donna Davis, your humor and skill at pointing out my comma and dash addictions helped me make this book sing; Michelle Drenick, for endless encouragement and countless adventures with our daughters so I could spend weekends writing; Merrin Stein and Katherine Dreyer, whose humor and wisdom in times of doubt is something I count on.

Sri Shambhavananda and your lineage of teachers, I will be indebted to you forever for teaching me the greater purpose of life and how to bring true spirituality into my daily life. To Jeanette, thank you for teaching me about the numbers long before I understood the role they would play in my life and work.

To all the students and clients I've worked with over the years, this book is the result of everything you taught me. Thank you for your stories, feedback, suggestions, and encouragement, which were essential for my learning. Thank you, Naropa University, for bringing my work to your classrooms long before anyone else; and *Nexus: Colorado's Holistic Journal,* for publishing my monthly columns.

My gratitude goes out to Kai, my stepson, whose sweetness and brilliance inspires me to learn and laugh on this great adventure we've signed up for.

I'd like to pay tribute to my amazing mother, my first teacher, and the one who passed along the powerful intuitive gift that guides this book and my life.

And finally to my daughter, Sarah. You are the inspiration behind all that I do. May you grow up understanding that it's all on purpose, the good and the bad, and it's getting you exactly where you intended to go in this lifetime—using your boundless gifts to help raise the consciousness of the planet.

PREFACE

Are You On Path?

Did you know that you arrived on Earth with a GPS device embedded inside you? You programmed it before you were born. It contains all the directions you'll ever need in this lifetime. It's designed to get you dead on target to your destined great work—the work you came here to do that uses your talents to raise the vibration of the planet in your unique way.

Even when your life feels as if it's not moving forward, as if your career is slipping through your fingers, as if relationships you used to count on are shifting—you will move through this phase and emerge at the other end with a more powerful direction than ever before.

You're just getting a little nudge from the universe, which is telling you it's time to get back on path. Nudging is what's going on when you get fired, laid off, rejected, hired, promoted, or your business goes bankrupt. *You've been nudged!*

Your life is on purpose. There are no accidents. Every event, circumstance, and relationship has been nudging you to follow your true path and do your great work—which is the only path to real success and abundance.

When your work is in alignment with your mission—you prosper—against all odds.

Before you were born your soul knew what it needed to do in order to evolve to its highest good; you knew that as you evolved you would help thousands of people around you evolve. You signed up for this human adventure in order to help all of humanity.

You understood that you could choose to live up to your fullest potential, use your energy to master circumstances, and use your talents to raise the vibration of the planet through your great work. Or you could give in to depression, sadness, anger, fear, and desperation—and not live up to the powerful divine potential you set for yourself. It would be your choice.

You also knew that only when your work was in alignment with your true mission would you attract success and abundance—no matter how bad the economy was, how few jobs were available, or how many people told you that you would never succeed.

You signed up for this!

And now here you are. At the office party your boss announces that your company is downsizing and won't need your services anymore; your spouse leaves you for a dancer; and your real estate and stock market investments flop.

Say, Thank you! I must have been really off my true path to get kicked this hard. Turn around and face forward. Ask yourself, What do I want my life to look like now?

Take one step in that new direction. You'll feel better immediately.

When we've fallen off our true path, our loved ones get fed up with us, bosses fire us, coworkers complain about us, and we stop attracting clients and customers.

If you've just been nudged, wake up. You're not a victim. You're being reminded that you need to go in a direction that's closer to your true self, your naked self, and the divine work you came here to do. (If you don't listen, the nudging will only get worse).

We live in a world of constantly changing cycles. When you're done with one cycle, it's done with you. Move on, so the universe doesn't have to kick you in the butt.

When everything is slipping through your fingers, let it go. When you've lost a job, let it go. Come up for air, and look around you at the big picture of your life. Ask: What did I really come here to do? (It's always bigger, better, and more meaningful than what you've been doing.)

Wouldn't it be better if the world didn't have to nudge you (sometimes painfully) to get on path? Wouldn't you prefer to see the road yourself and move forward through its twists and turns fearlessly— along the journey you already signed up for?

You can. This book gives you the tools to align your life with that original mission and succeed—whether you're launching a first career or looking for that next career move. It will show you how to listen to your inner GPS unit (also known as intuition) saying, "Turn left," or "Forge straight ahead."

Tapping into your intuition will reveal the quiet dreams, desires, and wisdom that you've stuffed away to fit in—especially if you've spent years working in a corporate environment.

In addition I'll share with you the ancient wisdom that will shed a powerful light on your search for meaningful work and answer the timeless question, Why am I here? Written from my experiences as a career intuitive, medium, and numerologist, this book will illuminate your career path, explain your dreams and longings, and make sense of your deepest pain. By the time you finish reading, you'll be back in touch with that real you—the naked you who came here on purpose.

You'll understand that your path is completely different from everyone else's. Your answers only come from within you—not from looking at what anyone else is up to. When you look at your neighbor and think, I want to do what he does for a living, you're forgetting your own unique journey—the one you chose long ago, which is probably very different from your neighbor's path. When you're not living true to what you signed up for, nothing works well—from relationships to finances.

But when you're firmly on your unique path, you feel impassioned by your life and work—no matter what anyone else is doing and no matter what anyone thinks of you. Abundance flows, and your life is in harmony.

I've studied and practiced this knowledge for more than thirty years. I've witnessed its truth in my life and seen it save the lives of countless clients. I know beyond any shadow of a doubt that it can change your life. It provides a larger, empowering perspective that's missing from other career books.

The powerful steps outlined in these next pages are designed to help you own up to your unique chosen path—with your pain fueling you and your gifts guiding your direction. I'll teach you how to decode your life's mission and tap into your own intuitive guidance system.

I'll share the stories of clients who've turned their lives around, and I'll share my personal journey of owning up to my intuitive gifts. By the end of this book you'll have the knowledge, the practical tools, and the inner guidance system to manifest your true destiny work—which is your only path to real success and abundance.

INTRODUCTION:
A MESSAGE FROM BEYOND

I T'S 2 A.M., AND I'm sound asleep when suddenly there's a strange and very large man standing right beside my bed—about a foot away. He's wearing jeans, a dark T-shirt, and an unbuttoned plaid flannel shirt. He's not trying to scare me; he's just casually standing there looking at me—rather sweetly.

But he does scare me; it's the middle of the night and I don't know him. As my sleepy brain processes all this information, I'm already screaming, "Who are you?" and struggling to sit up in bed.

Now my husband, our two kids, the cat, and the dog are all wide awake—yelling, "What's wrong?" and making lots of commotion. But I don't notice them, because I'm still seeing this man beside the bed—quite clearly—even as I sit up and even as my husband turns on the light. Only then does the stranger very slowly, lingeringly, almost cell by cell, vaporize in front of me. There's a slight crackling sound as his form disappears before my eyes.

"It's just a dream. Go back to sleep," my husband, Gene, says. But I can't go back to sleep. I can't believe he wasn't a real flesh-and-blood person standing there.

"You didn't see anybody standing by the bed?" I demand. But Gene is chuckling—laughing at me. "Sue, you need to be nicer to these spirits. You invite them to give you messages for clients, and when they get here you yell at them." He's still laughing as he turns off the light and slides back down against his pillow—snoring peacefully within seconds.

I am wide awake and confused now—pacing in the bedroom, opening closet doors, checking hallways. Certainly this man was real flesh and blood, a burglar. I saw him so clearly! Are the doors locked?

I never get back to sleep that night as I run this image through my mind over and over. I'm used to precognitive dreams, yes, and even seeing the quick flashes of spirits with their messages for loved ones. But this was something else—this was right out of *Star Trek*. This was a complete, solid apparition, just inches from my face.

In the morning when the alarm rings, it's back to being Mom, making breakfast, driving the kids to school, and then a phone session with a new client from New Orleans named Elizabeth. Before the phone session I meditate on her life and career path, which I pick up from the vibrations of the numbers in her birthday. I can see how powerful she is—a large and magnificent spirit here to do something great. I'm excited to work with her.

Later, as we're talking, I can tell she's fallen off path—not quite living up to the big work she came here to do. She's running a business that's frustrating her, and there are other disappointments weighing her down. Her voice sounds tired.

She tells me the story of losing her young daughter to an illness twenty years earlier. "I lost my faith in life then," she remembers. She tells me about meeting Jim, a man with a large spirit and generous heart who became her best friend, mentor, and business partner. Together they discussed the big questions of life: Why are we here? Where do we go when we die? Is there an afterlife?

These discussions comforted Elizabeth because she wanted to

know that her daughter's spirit did indeed exist in an afterlife—where she might find her again someday. Elizabeth and Jim made a promise to each other: Whichever of them dies first will return with a sign to show the other that there is indeed an afterlife.

Tragically Jim dies of a heart attack not long after they've made their promise to each other. Elizabeth waits and looks for a sign but sees nothing. This saddens her deeply as she tries to live with the belief that there is no afterlife, no spirit life—just this seen "reality" in which we exist day to day. This weighs on her—causing depression. What purpose is there in this meaningless existence, she wonders?

While Elizabeth is telling me this story, I'm jumping off my chair saying, "Wait, wait—let me describe Jim to you!" I describe the man standing beside my bed, whom I can still see in great detail—down to his large belly and gray hair. I explain how kind and good he seemed—not trying to scare me—but putting tremendous effort into materializing before my eyes, so that I would not forget him, so that I would not go back to sleep, so that I would remember to tell Elizabeth when we talked in the morning. I can feel the great love he has for Elizabeth and the energy he poured into getting this message to her.

As I tell her this I can hear her crying. "Really? Do you believe that?" she asks. "That was really Jim?"

I can feel Jim beside me now, urging me on. "Elizabeth, if I can tell you anything that I know is absolutely true, it's that Jim desperately wants you to know there's an afterlife and that the spirit world is real." She is sobbing when we hang up.

Over the next few months we do more phone sessions and create a plan for lining up Elizabeth's work with the intention of her birth path—the refined and highly spiritual vibration of the number 7. She needs work that allows her to use her great ability to synthesize knowledge and meaning and then to share that higher understanding with others—through teaching, writing, and counseling. Her ultimate path will be realized when she's translating the highest spiritual wisdom for others and helping them see their lives in more enlightened ways.

Through discussions about the pain of losing her daughter, the mission of her birth path, and where she is in the cycle of her journey (personal year), she makes a list of baby steps to take toward manifesting this important new work.

Months later I meet Elizabeth in person. She tells me how important the message from Jim was, and how it's reopened her ideas of what life is about and why we're here. "I'm getting back in touch with my spirituality," she tells me. And she's been taking baby steps toward a new career: "I'm enrolled in classes, and I'm doing some writing."

I'm very relieved to know that this powerful, beautiful woman, on an important journey in this lifetime, is back on path—realigning her life and work to be more in harmony with her mission.

I remember the dark years after my husband died when I was twenty-nine and fell off path—not doing my true work or being my true self. I'm deeply grateful to the people who nudged me back on path to the work I came here to do.

PART

I

HOW
I SEE YOUR
DREAM JOB

I

GROWING UP IN
THE CITY OF SPIRITS—
NEW ORLEANS

I'M A CAREER INTUITIVE, a medium, and I see dream jobs. When I work with clients I see their gifts and potentials: what they came here to do, the careers they would love, and where they should live. This information comes to me as photographic images, auditory messages, and powerful sensory feelings that I transmit directly to my clients. Sometimes I see my clients' departed loved ones, who come to the session to offer career guidance.

This joining of two seemingly disconnected worlds—the divine realms and the world of work—seems to be my particular talent. I was born in New Orleans to a French Cajun mother who came from a long line of women with "the gift." I inherited a double dose of telepathy, clairvoyance, and precognition from her and her mother, and back through generations of her family—the Degas women (whether we're related to the famous artist, we're not sure).

These unusual gifts were nurtured by the mysterious city of my childhood. In the haunted alleys of the French Quarter, almost everybody gives respect to the "unseen" world in some form or other—whether it's through voodoo, Catholicism, psychics, vampires, or Mardi Gras.

My early years were flavored with this spicy magic—from my grandpa's stories of the swirling Mississippi River to the unforgettable images I absorbed in the dark recesses of Crescent City life. I thrived on the rhythms of my crazy Cajun ancestors.

Like them, I heard other people's thoughts and had too-vivid dreams of events that would happen in the future. Sometimes this was helpful; mostly it just contributed to my "nerdy" childhood. In first grade, when the school bully had me cornered behind a building, I spoke his thoughts out loud, and he took off running as if he'd seen a ghost. In high school I dreamed the exact details of a car wreck and was able to prevent it from happening the next day.

For most of my childhood I was sensitive to these other realms—whether I wanted to be or not. And trust me, I didn't want to be! Being psychic was not "cool" in the fifties; it was more "crazy" than cool, and didn't want to be crazy. Gidget wasn't crazy, and neither was Hayley Mills. In the days of Marilyn Monroe and Elvis Presley, ponytails and sock hops, normal was in. That's all I aspired to be.

Southern girls from middle-class Catholic families weren't allowed the luxury of psychic powers. When I talked about things I had dreamed that came true, people left the room; they told me I had an overactive imagination. I lost friends. So I learned to keep it to myself.

But the dreams were relentless; I dreaded going to sleep because it meant entering an alternate reality of precognitive dreams and astral travel that was terrifying for a kid. Today I would be diagnosed with "night terrors" and given drugs to knock me out. But in the fifties I was on my own. So I taught myself to pray the Our Father incessantly—even during my sleep.

As a child I took great comfort in Catholicism's rituals and saints. In that world my dreams were nearly acceptable. I prayed fervently to the Virgin Mary during mass—which attracted the admiration of my third-grade teacher, Sister Mary Leo. She took me aside and said I was well suited for the "religious life," meaning that I would be a good nun (or nerd—my interpretation).

The idea of convent life was strangely comforting—until seventh grade, when I saw the Beatles perform on the *Ed Sullivan Show*. From then on my future was clear—I would marry Paul McCartney.

My mom's Cajun family had a long tradition of intuitives. Yet these powerful strong-willed women kept pretty quiet about their dreams and their ability to know what was happening to faraway loved ones, until we got together for family gatherings. Then I heard the whispered stories of dreams that came true and of waking in the night knowing when someone had died—before the phone rang to bring the news.

Besides passing along the gift, my mother supplied me with a most essential tool: unflinching determination. Without her tremendous strength I would have gotten lost in the confusing world of telepathy and clairvoyance. Mom's message was clear: Fit in, be strong, and have a conventional life. There were *no* options.

I kept the dreams and visions to myself. I knew that I had the power to see the other world, but I saw no good reason to do so. It would only cause trouble. And, hey, Gidget never saw spirits or had weird dreams. Neither did Paul McCartney. And, as my mother pointed out, talking about this stuff could get me a stint in the local mental hospital.

Meanwhile the dreams continued. We spent summers at our beach house in Long Beach, Mississippi, where I often woke the family with piercing screams about the wall of water washing over our house and sweeping away everything we owned. This vivid precognitive dream was repeated throughout most of my childhood. My brothers learned to throw a pillow at my head before the screams could wake our baby sister.

But the dreams made my grandfather uneasy. He had weathered numerous hurricanes in the house and was confident that our home was built like a fort. Yet as I got older, he would ask for more details of the dream, which I would relate as best I could.

One night, when we were sharing stories, he put his hand into the moonlight shining through our window. "You see that light, Sue Ellen. That's perpetual light—that's what God is. And God is always with us."

That simple conversation became the foundation for my lifelong understanding of God as ever-present divine light. This awareness helped calm the fears that my dreams inspired.

The summer I turned seventeen, in 1969, Hurricane Camille sent a thirty-foot wall of water over our Long Beach house and left nothing but the concrete foundation. We had evacuated, so no one was hurt. But the loss of Long Beach was a trauma from which our family never fully recovered. It marked a turning point in my life; I left for college that same summer and seldom came home again.

Another recurring dream was of seeing the city of New Orleans under water. In the dream I was in a car with my family on a city street, and suddenly we were submerged under five feet of water. Or we would be driving across the Lake Ponchartrain Causeway when the road would disappear into the water, and we would drive off the edge.

In 2005 Hurricane Katrina destroyed the city and the Lake Ponchartrain Causeway exactly as I had seen it in my dreams for thirty years.

When I got pregnant at the age of forty-two, I dreamed of my unborn child—who told me her name was Sarah and that she really loved me. I saw her perfect face as clear as a photo, and it's the exact face that I see today when I look at her.

My psychic gift is most powerful now that I use it to help others. The precognitive images that I see help me guide my clients to their true work. But it took me more than fifty years to embrace this ability to see the unseen world and learn what it had to teach—rather than being ashamed or afraid of it.

2

THE DEATH THAT
WOKE MY SPIRIT

O NE OF MY STRONGEST EXPERIENCES in confirming the power of the unseen realms began in 1978, when I met and married a fellow mountaineer, Paul Frederick. We were both mountaineering instructors, crazy in love and planning a family when he was diagnosed with colon cancer and given two weeks to live.

From the moment of his diagnosis, we were determined to overcome it. Paul, who was only thirty-five, would survive. We explored conventional and alternative healing methods; Paul went through two surgeries to remove tumors from his colon and several rounds of chemotherapy. This conventional approach made little difference as the cancer spread, and we quickly became immersed in energy work, visualization, herbal medicine, and Native American medicine. Paul was part Cherokee, so his mother and sister provided us with books and healers from the Native American tradition. They got us an audience with a famous Sioux healer, Chief Fools Crow.

Over the next few months (even though Paul was given only two weeks to live, he lived exactly one year from the date of his diagnosis—July 13), as Paul's health deteriorated, I experienced many extraordinary other-realm experiences with him. Chief Fools Crow became Paul's constant dream companion. Paul awoke each morning with a new story to report about something Fools Crow had taught him the night before. The most dramatic was Paul's sudden ability to speak Lakota—the language of the Sioux.

In the last few weeks before he died, Paul woke up singing a Lakota death song every morning. He said Fools Crow taught him two songs—one to deal with the pain and one to help him die. When the doctors heard this strange singing, they thought he was either speaking in tongues or was delirious, and they reported this in his medical charts. In college I had studied Native American history and was very familiar with the language of Lakota. I knew exactly what he was singing.

On a rainy summer day in July 1980, Paul slipped into a coma. For nearly twenty-four hours the accumulated stress of the past year washed over me in waves of nausea. Eventually I fell asleep on the floor. As soon as I dozed off, Paul appeared in front of me. He was smiling and quite happy. He touched my arm and said, "Don't worry. I'm free. But what are you waiting for? You said I could die in your arms."

I awoke with a jolt and cleared everyone out of the room. Paul's mother and I stood on either side of him. We rubbed his arms and legs and told him it was okay to go now—that we wanted him to be free. We told him to leave his body and fly out into the soothing summer rainstorm.

As soon as we spoke those words, Paul's breathing changed for the first time in forty-eight hours. He took one long peaceful sigh, and his spirit left his body. I saw it leave as clearly as you can see your hand in front of your face. It was an image I'll never forget. It was Paul's gift to me.

I would never again doubt the spirit world or my ability to see it. That final moment was a confirmation of what I was here to do. I realized for the first time that we (our souls, not our conscious minds) are in charge of how and when we die—even how and when we take our last breaths. And I knew with every cell in my body that death was only a passage of the spirit into the unseen realms.

A few years later my best childhood girlfriend, Crissie, died after a two-year bout with leukemia. A decade later my father died one month after being diagnosed with lung cancer. I wasn't able to be with either of them when they died (I had just left the hospital to pick up my daughter from the babysitter when my father passed, and Crissie and I had spent a heartfelt time together just weeks before her death). Yet they both appeared and spoke to me at the moment of crossing over.

By this time I was clear beyond all doubt that we are spiritual beings having a human experience—rather than the other way around—and that we've come here on a mission. Eventually I understood that my work was to help people remember that.

Today I'm abundantly grateful for my work, which is my passion. My intuitive gifts are finally out of the closet, and I'm able to share them freely with others. The images and dreams that have always guided me are now guiding others through my work as a professional career intuitive.

3

HOW CLIENTS
REVEALED MY GIFTS

IN THE YEAR 2000, after a long journalism career as a health writer (spurred by Paul's death), I launched my business as a career coach. I planned to do traditional career counseling the way I had been trained at University of Missouri thirty years earlier. And at first I did. But the more clients I had, the more relaxed and open I became—which allowed my intuition to blossom. Soon I was amazed and baffled by the images and information that came to me during my work with clients.

While we calmly discussed job searches and résumés, vivid photographic images of my clients working in certain types of settings (such as being a pilot, teaching in a classroom, or being a detective) flashed before me. What did these images mean?

When I asked clients if they had ever worked in those specific careers, I found out that these were the hidden dream careers they hadn't had the courage to pursue or even tell anyone about. Yet these were the careers that excited them most.

For example, Roy, a depressed software engineer, dreamed of being in the FBI but was in his early thirties and thought it would be impossible to get accepted. He came to see me in the unhappy pursuit of yet another engineering job. While he sat miserably describing his dreary cubicle working conditions and oppressive daily tasks, I saw colorful images of him chasing someone through dark alleyways and working in an office with a large government seal on the wall.

When asked about this vision, Roy shyly admitted that he had always dreamed of working for the FBI. His whole being lit up with excitement as he talked about this secret dream. We worked for months to move his life in that direction and overcome the negative beliefs that sabotaged his efforts to pursue this lifelong dream. Today he's a successful student at the FBI academy and loves his new life.

Other times, written words and impressions appeared above my clients' heads. For example, John, CEO of a retail business, lived in Denver with his wife, who worked in the medical field, and their four-year-old daughter. He and his wife were both unhappy with their work—which was hurting family life. They were contemplating divorce. From the first time I worked with John, the word "Vail" kept popping into my visual field.

When I mentioned it, he explained that he longed to move his family to Vail but didn't think they could make a living there. He was afraid to even mention this dream to his wife, because she would tell him it was unrealistic. After a little intuitive career coaching, he and his family now live and work happily in Vail. She's a fabulously successful high-end realtor, and he's the CEO of an international corporate consulting company. Their marriage is better than ever, and their young daughter is becoming an accomplished ski racer.

The strangest occurrences were when the spirits of departed loved ones began showing up during sessions. For example, as Craig described his job unhappiness at a large corporation where he was a project manager, a young girl with straight blond hair, bangs, and blue eyes made herself visible to me beside him.

When I asked Craig about her, he said his wife had blond hair and blue eyes. I told him I was sure his wife hadn't come to the session in spirit form, because she was very much alive. Then he reluctantly told me a tragic story about his younger sister, who was killed in a car accident when he was in his early twenties. Craig brought an old photo of her to our next session, and I could see she was exactly who was showing up beside him.

As we worked, it became clear that his sister, even though she had died more than twenty years earlier, had a message for Craig to follow his dreams of being a teacher. She was quite insistent about it, in fact. This divine guidance from his sister helped Craig find the courage to change career direction. He was deeply moved to know that, after all this time, his sister still cared about his happiness and wanted him to pursue his dreams.

After that I openly invited departed loved ones to show up for my clients, and they did. Several clients, who (unknown to me) had just lost a parent or spouse, were inexplicably drawn to work with me. Their departed loved ones offered wise career advice and urged them to pursue their dreams. They made it clear that we come here to fulfill our dreams, which guide us to our mission, and that our happiness depends on accomplishing what we came here to accomplish.

I also learned to pay close attention to my sleeping dreams and how they might apply to clients. If someone from the other realms had an important message for a loved one, he or she would sometimes come through to me the night before our session.

(Note: If you'd like to understand how the birth-path system works, turn to chapter 7. If you want to read the stories of how other people changed their lives, then read on.)

In a dream . . .

He's a thin man, a cowboy in tight jeans, standing in front of me with his hands in his pockets. We're having a conversation when I realize that he's dying; he has advanced cancer and is pretending not to know it.

"You need to go into the hospital," I explain. "Well, I don't really want to do that," he says casually. I become concerned about this man not getting help, and I visit a hospital, walking down its long corridors, trying to find someone or an empty room.

Walking behind me very slowly, he whispers, "Tell her to write. I'm sorry about the cancer." I turn around and he has died, slipped away in front of me before I could find help.

I wake up.

I don't know him. It makes no sense. Who was he? I rack my brain for connections. Sleepy, I drive the kids to school, get a latte, and come home to meditate on my first client before I call her.

It's hard to get a reading on Cathy. She's a down-to-earth Capricorn on the path of the "hardworking number 4." And, I realize, as I look at the birth date she sent me, that so is her husband. They're both earthy and practical—very strong and intensely bound to each other.

In her e-mail she said he had died last summer. I can feel that he was powerfully grounded and worked with his hands. And it's clear, from meditating on her birth date, that she needs meaningful work to ground her—to give her purpose—even though she's financially comfortable from the money her husband left her.

As I meditate on both of them, I realize that he's the dying man in my dream telling me that he's "sorry about the cancer." I ask him now what he wants me to tell Cathy, and the words come: "I provided for her. She's okay. Tell her not to be so upset. Tell her to relax. I don't know why she's so upset." I write all this down for my client.

Cathy's having a rough time and cries from the moment we begin talking. She tells me that she was recently hospitalized for depression, and she's falling apart. I tell her I had a dream, and it might be her husband. She takes a deep breath and gets quiet. "Okay, tell me."

I describe the down-to-earth man in the dream. I tell her he knew he was sick but didn't want the medical care. He wanted it to go the way it went. He's sorry that it traumatized her. But he's okay now and wants her to be, too. Again the words "Tell her to write."

"Yes, he had stomach cancer and died a couple weeks after he was diagnosed," she explains. "Died at home . . . never lost consciousness until the end. He suffered terribly."

She is devastated by the loss and more devastated by the memory of the suffering he went through while she cared for him. "He was my rock. I can't go on without him. I'm traumatized by it."

I give her all his messages. I remind her how strong she is and that she chose this experience as part of her journey. "He wants you to relax and enjoy your life. But I think you need meaningful work to ground you."

"Yes, I feel so lost. My job is meaningless."

Cathy explains that she and her husband were National Park Service rangers for twenty years. I'm amazed at how well that reflects their chosen paths, combining the earthy Capricorn energy with the physically strong path of the number 4; a perfect expression of destined work for these two hardworking soul mates. And now he's gone.

Last summer Cathy transferred to a desk job doing administrative tasks for the Park Service. She can't go back to being a ranger without him, yet the administrative work is meaningless.

"What did he mean about the writing?" I ask.

"I wrote a blog about what my husband was going through last summer, and people loved it. They said I was a great writer. My husband always told me I should write professionally."

"Have you explored a writing career?" I ask.

She says she hasn't, so we discuss ideas, classes, books to read, projects to start. Slowly her voice becomes more alive—in small bits—like an engine starting to catch after a long hard winter. I feel her husband beside me nodding in approval. "Yes, yes," he says. "Tell her to write."

Before we hang up, she's promising to follow up with the assignments we discussed, taking classes, reading books, looking into graduate schools. There's hope in her voice. I remind her that she's still here on purpose with something meaningful to do. "Your pain is your fuel," I explain. "Use it now to make the world a better place."

After the session I thank her husband for showing up and offering guidance. I tell him I hope we got it right.

Sometimes when we're in grief, the only guidance we'll accept is what comes from our departed loved ones. He got through to her this time, and she may have turned a corner in her grieving process. My hope is that she'll rally her strength to move forward. I hold that vision for her.

Months later she contacts me and says she has submitted articles to a local magazine, and they're being published. She's so excited about this affirmation of her writing abilities that she's sending out more articles to other publications. She's also taking evening writing classes at her local college. As we talk I can hear in her voice that her spirit is renewed, alive again. She has tapped into the passion for a new career that is truly on path for her. Her departed husband helped save her life. I'm grateful for being the messenger.

4

A POWERFUL ANCIENT SYSTEM TO HELP YOU FIND YOUR PATH

THIS UNUSUAL TECHNIQUE OF career counseling wasn't something that I was immediately comfortable with. I had spent years trying to prove I was realistic and practical and could fit into the conventional world, yet here I was seeing dead people and getting career guidance from them. My old pattern was to ignore these psychic experiences, but they were becoming impossible to ignore when working with clients.

About this time I had persistent dreams urging me to revisit another piece of knowledge from my past—my twenty-year study of numerology. This ancient system, founded in 580 B.C. by the mystic and philosopher Pythagoras, teaches that each number carries a meaning or vibration and that the numbers in our birth date and the letters in our name reveal our lifetime mission.

When my husband died in 1980, a girlfriend bought me a reading from a very gifted professional numerologist named Jeanette Howard. After reading my chart she decided to teach me everything she knew about numerology. According to Jeanette, I was destined for big work in the intuitive realms, and she wanted to pass along her numerology expertise to someone who would use this knowledge to do good work in the world.

Because of our sweet connection, Jeanette devoted much time, effort, and wisdom to my training. I still have several thick notebooks of information gathered during her tutelage. She believed it was my destined path to use this knowledge to help people.

I did have an instant knack for it. The deaths of my husband and best girlfriend had kicked me right into my intuitive powers, and Jeanette honed in on that. Enjoying our friendship, we studied, talked, did number assignments, shared books, compared charts, and kept up a steady dialogue of numerology study for more than ten years.

It was clear to Jeanette that my gift was especially suited for understanding birth paths, or what some called destiny numbers. The numbers revealed insights into many other areas of life, including relationships. But from the beginning I had an intuitive grasp of the different destinies we each choose to manifest in a lifetime and how to explain those destinies to people in a way that empowered them.

I had fun guessing the birth paths of people I met and later verifying that information with their birth dates. I kept dozens of notebooks filled with birth dates, career stories, and numerological insights. Not a day went by when I didn't study life in terms of how the numbers affect us.

Yet the power and truth that I discovered in these simple numbers disturbed me. I was again dabbling in the unseen realms and battling my survival urge to be grounded and practical. And the information was always right—which was very troubling. Were our destinies so clearly mapped out before a lifetime began? Where did that leave free choice?

Until the birth of my daughter in 1993, I did numerology charts for friends, family, and coworkers but wouldn't let anyone pay for them. I presented the knowledge lightly—to be taken with a grain of salt. Yet my colleagues found it helpful and often wanted more readings—which I declined.

Being a numerologist was not on my list of acceptable careers. I couldn't imagine telling my parents that I made my living doing something so "weird." Instead I made my living as a professional journalist—which made my family proud—and I was good at it. When my daughter was born I put away the numerology notebooks and focused on juggling motherhood and journalism, which was enough to keep me busy.

Years later, when I decided to use numbers to help me counsel clients, I was very cautious at first and only offered tidbits of insight about their chosen destiny paths. Yet these numerological insights clearly helped people make peace with their destined work and trust their own intuition.

To my surprise and relief, even the most conservative, successful corporate clients were enormously hungry for this deeper wisdom, and eagerly used the knowledge to evaluate career choices. Today I guide all clients with the insights gained from numbers because they provide an intuitive gateway that helps me connect to the person's mission.

Before my sessions I calculate the clients' birth path based on their birth date and study the combination of the birth path, sun sign (which describes the flavor of the work they've chosen to do), and the cycle of the personal year they're experiencing.

This potent combination of birth path and sun sign creates a gestalt impression of the work they came to do and the vibration of their mission. The personal year cycle they're being influenced by (also found in the birth date) reveals whether it's time to start something new, dig in and work hard, or let go of the old so a new career phase can begin.

I meditate on this information using an ancient Hindu-based technique. By quieting my mind through meditation, I enable impressions and images about the clients' path to come through as pictures, words, and feelings. I see the challenges and opportunities they're facing, as well as the great potential they came to live up to. I write it all down without censoring.

You can do this for your own life.

In chapter 7 I'll teach you a simple way to calculate your own birth-path number and use that information to guide your career. Numerology offers clear evidence of how we set up our lessons before we're born. I think you'll be astounded how well these destiny numbers reflect the choices you've made, or long to make, in your career. Combining that ancient knowledge with your own intuitive guidance will give you more direction than you'll get from taking dozens of career aptitude tests.

In chapter 19 I'll teach you the basics of meditation to quiet your mind, connect to your higher guidance, and help you move forward intuitively with your life and career.

If you've studied the law of attraction, which explains how positive energy attracts positive circumstances while negative energy attracts the bad stuff, you may be wondering how predestined life missions fit into the law of attraction.

For the past twenty years I've studied how these two philosophies intermingle and questioned how so many circumstances could be predestined if we live in a world that's based on free will and the law of attraction. After years of study and working with clients, I've come to understand how free will operates within this plan—as revealed through the numbers.

When we bump up against our predestined soul agreements (whether they're great opportunities or difficult challenges), our energy, and where it's focused, determines whether we rise to our great potential and overcome circumstances—or sink below our challenges and fail to live up to our potential.

We use our thoughts, beliefs, and feelings to make each moment better or worse, to pursue or sabotage each opportunity, and to rise to our greatest potential or wallow in our "pitiful" selves. It's up to each of us at every moment. And therein lies the free will and the power of our energy (thoughts, beliefs, and feelings) in this interactive universe.

When my beautiful, young husband, Paul, died a painful, too-early death from cancer, we were bumping up against a soul agreement we had made to go through that experience together in order to evolve spiritually. Our choice was in how we handled the challenge, the energy we brought to it, and the thoughts and beliefs I created about that event after Paul was gone.

Paul magnificently rose to his challenge—filling his spirit with love and light that transformed friends, family, and caretakers. His glowing, wise presence throughout the ordeal taught us all how to love and release him. His fully aware and conscious death was a gift to me.

After he was gone, my experience with Paul took me on a spiritual journey that culminated in a body of knowledge and wisdom that today allows me to help others move through their challenges.

This is the beauty of the grand plan. We have opportunity after opportunity to become the divine masters we came here to be—or delay our evolution by giving in to fear and desperation. The choice is yours. Your destiny numbers reveal how beautifully you've set up your journey.

In a dream . . .

I'm standing to the left of a splendidly tall, ancient wooden wall filled with intricate deeply carved Sanskrit letters. These letters fill lines and lines of the entire structure. I can't read what the ancient writing says, but I'm compelled to understand its meaning. I move closer and run my fingers across the carved Sanskrit. I become aware that behind the great wall is a deep valley of green forest expanding as far as I can see. The forest is silent and motionless, yet stunningly grand. It feels untouched by time and human existence.

"What do the carvings mean?" I ask out loud into the vast emptiness.

From behind me a voice says softly, "When we take the human incarnation, we're meant to move forward toward the light, to the soul, and not to dawdle or get distracted."

"How?" I ask.

I turn and see a deep, endless tunnel opening right in front of me. The tunnel appears to be limitless. From behind me a cat comes bounding out of nowhere and into the vast tunnel. At first it runs forward powerfully and with purpose. Then it slows down, stops, sits in the middle of the tunnel, and begins licking itself. It sees something small on the ground and knocks it around. The once-powerful cat now seems confused and directionless, not moving toward the end of the tunnel, focused only on the details.

I wake up.

Am I like the cat, I wonder? Am I dawdling, getting distracted, focused on the details, and licking myself when I should be moving toward the soul, toward the light? I vow to hone my work more powerfully to show my clients that their life stories are only the outer expressions of their souls' intended journeys—chosen before the lifetime—to use their gifts and pain to make the world a better place.

I vow again to remind people that their career choices can't be made from the influence of trends, fads, opportunities, or what others are doing. Their choices must come from the inner knowing, the intuition of the true naked self they came to share with the world. True abundance and success can only come from aligning ourselves with this naked work—the work that lines up with our pain, gifts, and dreams—our mission.

This is my true work—to share this knowledge of the soul's intention with others. It always has been, even though I buried my gift for many years trying to fit into conventional ways of making a living, trying to be accepted by others. (The cat licking itself in the tunnel . . .)

Yet I've always had this great gift, the missing filter, the dreams that take me directly to other realms for knowledge that I'm blessed to remember when I awake. All my life, when I've met people, I've seen them doing things, careers, that they're not yet doing.

For more than fifty years my logical, linear left hemisphere battled for dominance over this intuitive, all-knowing, wise right hemisphere that longed to meditate and dream—steeped in the knowledge of other realms. Now they've made peace with each other, and as the right hemisphere slowly takes dominance, I am allowed to see more and more of this information—being trusted to share it accurately with clients and students.

What's your story? Who are you really? Who is hiding inside you? It's time for all of us to come out of the closet and own up to who we really are. We're needed now to be our true, wise, intuitive selves as we guide humanity through this pivotal point in our evolution. Are you a healer who feels energy pulsing through your hands and yet you make your living as a lawyer? It's time to own your truth. By not following your gift, a life is wasted.

As money scares you into playing it dumb, please know that money follows only your true work. When you're on your true path, everyone around you feels that vibration of sacred alignment. You attract whatever and whomever you need.

I can't tell dreams from reality. I'm staring at a lake, a pool of vast deep water, still and glistening. Is this a dream or not? I'm under the water, swimming in a stream that is effortless, at home as in a place I've always known. I never want to leave this water. There are levels of it, like tiers that I swim up and up to get to the top of the endless pool.

At the top I emerge from the water feeling completely at peace and refreshed, and someone is standing there to meet me. He tells me sweetly that I can't be here yet, that I have more work to do. I argue with him. I'm crying when he taps me on the shoulder and I wake up. All day I can't shake the memory of the pools. I feel the joy of the water rushing over me. I smell it, hear it, taste it. Can I go there tonight in my sleep, or is an invitation required?

I am meditating on a client's path before I do a session with him. I see that he's an earthy Taurus on an expanded 5 birth path. I ask to be told what this client needs to hear to move forward to his highest potential. I see images of an attractive man with great material successes, surrounded by cars, homes, and other trappings of wealth. Yet he is careening into the abyss of addictions—sex and alcohol. What does he need from me? I ask.

The words come: reconnection to his spiritual path, a reminder of the soul's intention to teach and inspire others. He came to experience the greatest passions of human existence but got sidetracked into meaningless details and addictions.

I write it all down. I make a note to myself to be relentless in reminding him of his soul's journey, of waking him up to save his life. At the end of the session he says, "This is just what I needed. I don't want to hide anymore."

Months later he tells me he's become a corporate consultant who specializes in helping employees with addiction problems. He's also in graduate school getting his doctor of divinity so he can make his living as a spiritual counselor. His enormous gratitude and passion for his new direction fill me with happiness—lights me up. I say a prayer of gratitude.

TO SUMMARIZE THIS CHAPTER

◆ Started in 580 B.C. by the ancient mystic and philosopher Pythagoras, the founder of our number system, numerology teaches that each number carries a meaning or vibration and that encoded in each of our birth dates is the description of the destiny work we've come to share with the world.

◆ Combining the guidance available from numerology with your own intuitive guidance provides powerful direction in your life when facing career choices.

◆ When we bump up against our predestined opportunities or challenges, our energy and where it's focused determine whether we rise up to our great potential and overcome circumstances—or whether we sink below our challenges and fail to reach our potential.

5

YOU, TOO, CAN LEARN TO READ DESTINY

For as long as I can remember, I've been fascinated by the choices people make about their work. As an undergraduate at University of Missouri in the seventies, the campus career-counseling center was my favorite hangout, as well as my part-time job. Even when I wasn't "on the clock," I would show up and offer guidance to students exploring career directions. I couldn't explain how I "knew" what someone would be good at within a few minutes of meeting them. But I always did.

On weekends, while helping run career exploration workshops at the center, I loved the group discussions, interactive exercises, and aha! moments when students suddenly got clarity about their direction. It was all great fun.

Later, teaching mountaineering survival courses for Colorado Outward Bound School, I spent many evenings gathered around the fire or huddled under tarps listening to the students' life stories. Within a short time I could clearly see their gifts and talents and knew what they would love doing for a living. When I shared these insights, students were deeply grateful and kept in touch long after the course as they pursued career dreams.

When I started a career-counseling business in 2000, I became successful through word of mouth. My clients got what they wanted—clarity about career path and guidance to pursue it. Soon word spread that I worked "intuitively" and offered information from numbers that went beyond the usual career coaching. My client list quickly grew.

Over the years many clients have wanted to learn about the numbers themselves. They wanted to decipher their own code and understand the changing cycles of their lives and careers. So I shared the knowledge with anyone who wanted to learn it—through classes, workbooks, and sessions.

The good news is that anyone can learn the meaning of the numbers within your birth date and what they reveal about your career. You don't need to take dozens of career aptitude tests or spend thousands of dollars on coaching to find your next, most successful career move.

In fact, by the end of this book, you'll see your career choices in a new light. (You can thank Pythagoras for that.) Here's an example of how easy it is to learn.

ANNA'S STORY

Anna was a twenty-eight-year-old educational programming director at a well-respected small college. She worked with a team of five professionals to design adult learning programs that would attract new students and create academic excitement within the community. She loved education, providing new learning curriculums for students, and working with talented faculty.

The job should have been her dream job. But Anna was miserable. She hated the politics that caused bickering and pettiness and kept her from fully manifesting her exciting ideas. Since the college celebrated group consensus in decision making, she did not have final say on new ideas— even though she was nominally programming director.

As we worked together I helped her understand the turning point she had bumped into—her 9 personal year and her first Saturn returning (explained in chapter 10). This was a sign that change was required at this point in her life. The angst she felt was right on schedule. There was nothing wrong with her approach to the job or with her personality. It was simply time to change and do work that was closer to her true mission.

She confessed that it was a wonderful relief to know she could let go of her unhappy career and not think of herself as a failure. She would instead see this time as a necessary reinvention toward greater fulfillment and success in the future.

The new direction became more apparent when we discussed her birth path—as found in the numbers of her birth date (see chapter 7). On the path of the number 8 with Aries wrapped around it, she was born to lead and run the show herself. Working with a team would never be easy for her; she would feel unable to get things done. This made perfect sense. Since her path was all about learning to own her power and use it for good to create products and services for the world, feeling powerless was a true sign she was off path.

When she had final say in important matters, she would be working true to her path; power was what she came to learn about, and that power would have to be experienced through her career—one way or another. This helped her to realize that her frustrations with feeling powerless had caused her to participate in sabotaging behaviors at work (such as backstabbing and political power plays), which had only made things worse.

Her choice was clear: either change the cherished system of group consensus at her current workplace or find a new outlet that would allow her to take charge and learn the lessons inherent in her path.

"You're telling me what I've always known about myself but wouldn't own up to. I thought it was selfish to want to be in charge or to want to make lots of money doing something on my own," she confessed during our session. *"This is such a relief. It's a confirmation."*

Hungry for more knowledge about the numbers, Anna read everything she could get her hands on about numerology. I gave her workbooks like the one at the back of this book, and she analyzed the birth paths of people she knew and had worked with. This information gave her many "aha" moments and helped her see how and where she had veered away from her intuitive knowledge of the work she came here to do.

"From the time I was a kid, I would play business games," she explained. *"I designed my own Monopoly board at the age of six. I've always wanted to be the boss."*

As Anna reflected on how she had given away her power in career situations by doubting herself, she understood what steps were required next. Armed with this insight, Anna took charge. Over the next few months she researched an idea she had dreamed about for years—starting a small educational-content publishing house.

Her father had worked in publishing, and because of him she already knew a tremendous amount about the business. Combining that background with her love of educational products and books, she set about writing business plans, meeting with investors, and brainstorming with her dad about the business. The further she went with her plans, the happier she became.

"The challenges of starting my own business make me happier than the challenges of working for someone else. I've found my path, and even though I know it will evolve over time, I'm finally doing work that's in alignment with who I am."

Anna is still an avid student of the numbers and what they mean. At each decision point in launching her company, she asked herself if making that choice would be in alignment with her life mission or not. *"The number information is invaluable,"* she explains. *"I tell my friends, and practically anyone who'll listen, how to understand their own birth path and what that reveals about their career choices."*

TO SUMMARIZE THIS CHAPTER

◆ The ancient knowledge from numbers, simplified and updated in this book, will provide personal guidance for every aspect of your life.

◆ You don't need to take dozens of career aptitude tests, or spend thousands of dollars on coaching, to find your perfect career or your next career move.

◆ By understanding your birth path number as found in your birth date, you'll be able to make choices that put your career in alignment with what you came to accomplish.

◆ Your mission includes work that uses your talents to raise the vibration of the planet in your unique way.

6

PEOPLE JUST LIKE YOU WHO FOUND THEIR GREAT WORK

The Successful Man Who Couldn't Find a Job

THE MAN ON THE other end of the phone had a deep, gracious voice. I knew very little about him except that he was on the master soul path of 22/4 with the sun sign of Virgo wrapped around it. He wasn't here for mundane work; his power and charisma were on purpose—to help him bring inspired ideas to the world.

While meditating on his path, I saw that Joseph was here to bring the practical needs of everyday life into a higher, more enlightened vibration, to find solutions for day-to-day human struggles, and that it was big work—planetary work—that he had signed up to do. He was heading into his second Saturn returning (see chapter 10), which meant that he was fifty-eight and feeling a terrible angst about not having accomplished his mission.

This was an 8 personal year for him; career and money would be his primary focus now as he manifested the next great level of his work. It wasn't a year for hanging out and taking things easy.

During the session he explained that he had recently been let go after a successful corporate career with IBM, where he had enjoyed leading teams to create solutions for clients. This high-profile career had ended painfully when he was laid off due to budgetary cuts. Not happy with taking things easy, as his family urged him to do, he had applied for several similar jobs in the corporate world that he thought would be easy to land. However, he never got a serious offer through his attempts to find a new position.

I congratulated Joseph on manifesting such a powerful and clear career departure; now he had no choice but to do what he had signed up for—as revealed in the mission of his master soul birth path. All the experiences and knowledge from his former corporate career would serve him well in this next phase of work. We discussed his unspoken dreams and his childhood pain, both of which would fuel this great work.

"The things you are saying are incredible to me, Sue," he whispered. "I'm shaken up and tearful to think that the silent dreams I've had are on purpose. Everyone around me is telling me to enjoy my life now, relax and take it easy. I cannot do that."

Joseph's childhood story was powerful; his father had abandoned the family when Joseph was young. There were years of struggle and poverty. Joseph took great pride in being one of his first family members to attain a college degree (in engineering) and white-collar executive status.

When Joseph became an adult, he learned that his father had returned to his homeland in Africa years earlier. During the peak of his corporate success, Joseph traveled to his father's village to meet him. While there, they forged a new, healing relationship, and Joseph forgave his father for abandoning the family.

Joseph saw great suffering in his father's village. There was little food, and it was almost impossible to make a living. He became obsessed with the plight of these impoverished villagers, who blamed their troubles on government corruption.

"I met all these bright, intelligent people who could not see any solutions to their plight; they were lost in the vicious cycle of suffer-

ing and complaining about government inefficiencies. From my outside vantage point I could see new options. They had access to good
land and everything they needed for organic gardening in their own
backyards. I came home obsessed with the idea of helping them. But
I was still working at IBM, and I let it fall through the cracks. Most
people told me it was useless anyway, since the system had broken
down so badly."

We made a plan for Joseph to reconnect with some former business colleagues to discuss starting a nonprofit foundation that would
educate villagers about sustainable organic community-gardening techniques. The goal was to bring power and self-sufficiency back to each
village by supplying seeds, tools, and instruction.

We discussed ways to elicit corporate sponsorship from organic
food companies to make this dream real. Before we hung up Joseph said
he was moving forward to make it happen. Over the next few months
we did a few more phone sessions that focused on helping Joseph move
past his fear and create lists of practical next steps to take. Months later
I heard this from him:

"Sue, the things you reminded me of on the day of our first fate-
ful phone call launched me into a passionate mission that woke up
my heart and spirit from a long sleep. I'm happy to report that my efforts are flourishing. Through my connections with politicians and
business leaders, I am spearheading a project to teach and maintain
organic gardening techniques in small, impoverished African villages.
My goal is to help them become self-sufficient.

"We've run into the usual funding challenges, but I've recently
tapped into some great corporate sponsorship opportunities, and we
are moving ahead. It's the most meaningful work I've ever done, and
as the spokesman, I get to meet with corporate leaders and politicians to discuss our project. That's very rewarding."

HELEN'S STORY

From the sound of her voice on the phone, I could tell how strong and positively focused she was. Helen was a survivor, and she had done well with her life—building a successful career in medical sales that allowed her lots of time, freedom, and financial security. Yet at the age of forty-eight, she was tired, depressed, and confused. Even though she had a beautiful son and a loving partner, her life felt empty and pointless. Her confidence was slipping away. She felt as if she was losing herself.

But why was this happening? She had done all the right things.

Helen's path was the path of the number 6 wrapped in Aquarius. She was a born teacher-healer who was meant to teach new ideas that inspired others to live better lives. She had been drawn to medical sales intuitively knowing that she wanted to help people. Yet the sales aspect of it prevented her from having the hands-on satisfaction of knowing she had made a difference in someone's life.

Helen was in a 9 personal year, which meant this was a year of letting go and releasing the old, so she could start a new cycle and head in a better direction that was closer to her mission. In our first session we discussed her lifetime dream to do work that helped others, as well as her childhood struggles to survive in a challenging emotional climate. Her mom had gotten pregnant at a young age, and Helen had been raised by grandparents who had already raised a family of their own and had little energy for another child.

"I learned not to make any trouble," she explained. So she hadn't. Following a conventional career path that didn't require much higher education, Helen launched a sales career that helped her become financially independent as quickly as possible.

We worked together for several months, and Helen learned to let go of old negative patterns of fear and self-doubt that were holding her back. "I had to learn that it was okay to focus on my needs and take a stand for what I wanted. I realized I had a responsibility to live up to my highest potential, and not just get by."

She forged a plan to return to school and finally become the therapist she had always wanted to be. She cut back her hours at work while she pursued her counseling degree. She also took classes toward becoming a Methodist minister, part of her lifetime dream to help others.

Since she was on the 6 path, she had fallen into the trap of surrendering her own needs to the needs of those around her—including her partner and son. By sharing her pain and unhappiness honestly with them, they rallied to her support, helping her make a smooth career transition.

SAM'S STORY

Sam was on the path of the expansive, charismatic number 5 with Leo wrapped around it. Anything short of being onstage in front of thousands of people was never going to satisfy him. But he had already learned that. At the age of forty-seven, with a successful career in sales for a high-tech company, he had hit the wall. Feeling bored and adrift, he had begun developing a side business as a life coach. Now he was torn between these two directions and had called me for guidance.

"Do I walk away from this lucrative sales career that other people would kill for? The economy is awful. What if I give up this secure job and my business as a coach never takes off?" he asked during our first session.

Sam's 5 birth path explained his need to live fearlessly and passionately. He needed adventure and freedom in his work to feel alive. He was heading into a new cycle of his career; it was time to turn around and share his fearlessness with others. "So I guess that explains why I feel so trapped in my current job, and why I've started planning a workshop called Beyond Freedom."

We both laughed. "It's my job to tell you what you already know and give you the courage to follow your intuition," I explained.

Sam's life story had been one of overcoming addictions (very common for anyone on a 5 path mission). His powerful personal charisma had helped him succeed in sales, where he thrived on travel and meeting new people. Yet he was most proud of recovering from alcohol and sex addictions to build a strong, healthy relationship with his wife and children.

"Now I want to share my story with others and help them see that if I can do it, they can too," he said.

"That's very much on-path work for you," I told him. With his Leo sun sign giving him tremendous warmth and charisma, and his passionate life story to tell, he could help many others break through their fears. If he marketed his coaching business accurately by focusing on his unique gifts and the clients who would most benefit from his message, he would thrive financially—no matter how troubled the economy was.

Over the next few months, Sam slowly built his coaching business, wrote his life story as a self-published book to sell online, and built a Web site announcing his coaching practice and upcoming workshops. With a strong background in sales and marketing, he knew how to generate interest in what he had to sell. And he did.

Through his first workshop he generated enough income from attendance and book sales that his wife realized the financial potential of what he had to offer. "She told me to quit my sales job," he said incredulously during a session. "I was so afraid she wouldn't believe I could do this."

By the time he walked away from his sales job, he had developed a reliable stream of income through coaching, teaching workshops, and selling books online. Today he is happier, healthier, and not at all bored. He's very good at what he does because it's his mission—what he came here

to do. *Success follows anyone who aligns their work with their true mis-*
sion. Sam's story is a great example of that.

HANS'S STORY

Hans had a successful high-profile marketing and advertising career in New York City. He had worked on several ad campaigns for huge retail companies as well as Broadway productions. He made a good living enjoying the Manhattan lifestyle with his partner. But at the age of forty-one, he found his work meaningless and empty.

During our session he told me that in recent years he had experienced several humbling "disasters" in his career that had resulted in his being laid off by the prestigious firm where he worked. His friends, who recognized his tremendous talent and experience, encouraged him to jump back in and apply for even better marketing positions. But his heart wasn't in it. He got no response from the places where he applied. A study of his birth path and the cycle of his personal year revealed the problem.

He was on the path of the number 9 with Aquarius wrapped around it. He needed a sense of meaning, humanitarianism, and service to others— an involvement in solving the problems of the world—in order to be fulfilled. Yes, he had tremendous creative talent and brilliance, but he had taken that as far into marketing as his spirit would let him.

"I really hate what I do," he confessed. "I'm using my talent to find ways to manipulate the public into buying something. And yes, I'm very good at it. But my attitude has gotten worse and worse in the last few years."

Upon reflection Hans knew that he had caused his own career "disasters" with his negative attitude. And he realized that four years ago (during *his 9 personal year), he had known it was time to change direction. At that time he lost a marketing job he adored because a larger firm bought his company and fired him and many of his colleagues.*

"I had been inspired and happy to go to work there before the takeover. When the management changed and I lost that job, I looked into a new direction but didn't have the courage to pursue it. Since then the places I've worked haven't been positive environments for me. I haven't done well."

Because he had lacked the courage to change when he went through the end of his nine-year cycle (see chapter 10), he had dragged his old career into the new cycle, with painful results. I explained that it was never too late to change, and, in fact, he was now in a 5 personal year, which meant that new opportunities would appear to help him discover a new career direction.

In my meditation for him before the session, I had received guidance that he could serve humanity by helping find alternative fuel solutions or by teaching adults new ways of healthy living. When I shared this with him, he laughed. He had a Ph.D. in chemistry and had originally taught and studied alternative fuel sources at a German university. But he had moved to New York from Germany after getting his Ph.D., and life had taken him into marketing.

Together we examined his life mission and where that could take him next. We made a list of baby steps to pursue over the next few weeks, which included teaching science at a local university, teaching healthful cooking classes to adults (he had a passion for healthful, organic food), and becoming a lifestyle coach. He was relieved to understand why he felt so disillusioned with marketing.

Over the next few months Hans investigated all these directions. When we talked again, he told me that he was teaching culinary classes on weekends, and that he and his partner were running a small food business that delivered healthful lunches to Manhattan offices.. "I'm not yet on my big mission, but for now this is so much more rewarding. I get to teach people how to live healthier, greener lives and make food that helps them do that."

When we last spoke, Hans was getting his certification as a life coach and teaching part-time at a local university.

TO SUMMARIZE THIS CHAPTER

◆ No matter how successful or unsuccessful you've been so far in your career, understanding your birth path and personal year will explain when, why, and how to change or tweak directions.

◆ Navigating career change takes knowledge, courage, and help from an outsider who has no personal investment in your choices.

◆ The choice is not whether you work at a job you dislike to make good money or whether you work at something you love for little money. Once your work is in alignment with your true mission (as revealed by the numbers), your work will be successful and attract abundance—against all odds.

◆ When we're on path our vibration attracts what we need in order to thrive.

PART
2

FINDING YOUR INTENDED CAREER PATH

7

THE PATH YOU CHOSE

We're having tea—strong, sweet tea—as we sit on the stone veranda overlooking an emerald sea. You're laughing and telling funny stories about the challenges in your life, when the conversation turns to career. "I don't know—it's just not clear to me what my true work is or how to manifest it," you explain. "The job I'm doing—well, it pays the bills. But I feel like I'm dying inside."

We sip our tea and look quietly out over the stone wall beside our table—across the vast expanse of open water. There are white gulls in the distance, and a gentle breeze ruffles the cloth on our table.

"You're a master soul, my friend. You're required to own up to your great work in this lifetime," I whisper to you softly across the table. "Remember, you signed up for this. You chose to come forward as a teacher to use your gifts to help raise the vibration of the planet."

"I'm just not seeing it." You sigh with frustration, putting your cup down forcefully on its saucer. Again we pull out your notebook and look at your name, your birth date. We add the digits again and study the numbers. We meditate on your path.

"Yes, it's a master path," I explain. "No way around it. And yes, you wrapped that lovely Pisces energy around it to flavor your mission with emotion and intuition. It's quite a lovely path, actually, though different from what most people would call a 'normal' life."

"I guess that's the problem," you moan. "I see the path, but how do I do it? I have to pay the mortgage, and . . . the kids, well. That's another story. . . ."

"But you signed up for all that as well," I remind you. "Now you're bumping up against a big choice point in your life. What you do and think about right now determines everything. And it models a way of living for your children, who are watching every move you make and don't make."

"I get that," you say softly.

"Are you focused on the great possibilities in front of you, the potential solutions for making a change in your life? Or are you focused on the reasons why you can't change? Are you letting self-doubt and fear pull you down into the 'pitiful self,' where there are no solutions and steps can't be taken?"

"Guess I have been feeling kinda pitiful," you say with a smile. "I just don't feel good enough or smart enough to—I mean, who do I think I am to want to do something important in the world?"

"You are who you came here to be, and your mission is what it is. Don't waste your energy doubting it. Let's jot down some baby steps you can take to investigate doing the work we talked about. Let's see. You said you knew some people you could talk to about that business idea. And there were some Web sites you were going to visit and phone calls to make."

"But why do I have so much pain?" you ask. "It hasn't been an easy lifetime."

"You set it up that way. The pain in your lifetime is designed to become your fuel to do your work in the world—making the world a better place in your unique way. Your pain becomes your motivation—your mission."

"When I was growing up, I was abused and powerless," you explain. "I'm still wounded by that."

"It means your mission now is to offer to others what you wish had been offered to you; your work is to help others realize how powerful they are and learn to trust themselves and their own inner guidance—in spite of whatever circumstances make them doubt themselves."

"How?"

"By using your innate gifts in your work. Those gifts are always on purpose, not coincidental. They aren't supposed to be relegated to hobbies or volunteer work. We are meant to make our living with our gifts—not bury them."

"Then why am I so afraid?"

"Well, that's the 'pitiful self' that we all have—our universal negativity. We can choose to give in to our fear and not live up to our mission. Or we can choose to move forward anyway, using our fear as fuel to make us successful. At the end of our lifetime it matters to us how well we pushed past that fear and lived up to the mission."

You ponder that for a while as we finish the tea. Together we write a list of baby steps you can take to investigate your new career ideas, to move forward, to look into possibilities for change. You promise to focus your thoughts on solutions, and you promise to meditate or pray every day for at least twenty minutes in order to tap into your higher self and remember your mission.

We sit for a few more minutes in silence, watching the ripples in the water below us. After a while you say, "Okay, I'm good now. I remember." You stand up from the table. You wake up.

Imagine that you outlined your journey for this lifetime before you were born. Consider the possibility that you preprogrammed the challenges you're now facing in your life—with the intention of mastering these powerful lessons in order to live up to the great potential that lies untapped inside you.

This perfect life journey offers you the opportunity to use your gifts and pain as fuel to make the world a better place—if you choose to live up to it. (That choice is left to your free will.)

Your original plan was to be an inspired participant in the great human evolutionary adventure. You encoded this road map into the vibrations of the numbers of your birth date and name so that you could tap into that code whenever you needed to remember your destiny. Your greatest potential for this lifetime, your highest, most meaningful work is all clearly outlined in your name and birth date. (And yes, it's necessary to quiet the mind in order to tap into this inner guidance.)

This code vibrates inside you for a purpose. As you journey through your lifetime your birth code vibrates out a message to everyone you interact with. They sense your path not by the words you speak but by the vibrations they feel from you. And because of this code everyone around you is able to feel the intention of your lifetime and help you stay on track (by adding pain or pleasure to your journey).

That's what the ancient mystic and Greek philosopher Pythagoras, father of our modern number system, believed when, in 580 B.C., he designed a theory of numbers based on the digits 1 through 9. Pythagoras saw that everything in the universe operated in predictable cycles, and his basic units of measuring each cycle were these digits.

According to Pythagoras each number has a meaning or vibration, and by adding the numbers within your birth date and reducing them to single digits, you reveal the nature of the work you came here to do.

Today we still use the number system Pythagoras created, but we've disregarded the core meaning that was central to his system—that each number carries a meaning or vibration that goes beyond mere quantity.

In our left-brained world the higher meaning of numbers went out of favor as we embraced the linear, logical, quantitative values of numbers.

Yet numbers are our oldest symbols, and they're fundamentally linked to the abstraction of higher ideas. References to numbers having spiritual or metaphysical meanings can be found in every ancient civilization including those of the Egyptians, Chinese, Hindus, Hebrews (in the kabbalah), and early Christians. Even the Bible gives meanings to numbers in the book of Revelation.

In Pythagoras's system every number has a positive and negative vibration (which show its potential and challenges). Your destiny number, which is derived from your birth date, contains the vibrations of the greatness you came to achieve—along with the potential pitfalls of your path. By understanding this you can make better choices for your future.

To find the code for your journey, reduce all numbers to the digits 1 through 9—except for two cosmic vibrations, symbolized by the master numbers 11 and 22. These two numbers represent sacred birth paths designed to help humanity evolve. Thus, the numbers 11 and 22 are not reduced to single digits. All other numbers are reduced to 1 through 9 by adding the digits of the entire number together. For example, the number 43 equals 7 ($4 + 3 = 7$). And the number 20 equals 2 ($2 + 0$).

Every letter of the alphabet also corresponds to these numbers 1 through 9. For example, A = 1, B = 2, C = 3, etc.

Numerology reveals how you outlined your direction for this lifetime and chose the players in your drama (family, friends, and lovers) because they would push you past your limitations and help you rise to your potential. Nothing and no one in your life is an accident.

As you look back at your life and its ups and downs, realize that it was all on purpose to get you to this moment. You, your loved ones, even your enemies, are all coauthors of this grandly designed group evolutionary process.

Here's a general description of the positive and negative vibrations the numbers represent:

THE NUMBER 1

Positive aspects: Creativity; self-awareness; willpower; unique vision; forcefulness; individualism; leadership; independence.

Negative aspects: Loneliness; self-centeredness; arrogance; bossiness; lack of self-confidence.

THE NUMBER 2

Positive aspects: Intuition; connection; communication; understanding; sharing; mediation; love; patience; diplomacy; consideration; peacemaking; attention to detail.

Negative aspects: Dependency; loss of self; paranoia; hypersensitivity; cowardice; obsession with meaningless details.

THE NUMBER 3

Positive aspects: Entertaining; self-expression through writing, movement, or the arts; natural creativity; gifted communicator of ideas; playfulness; fun; beauty; charm; love of limelight; social graces.

Negative aspects: Conceited; coldhearted; overintellectual; antisocial; verbose; superficial; jealous; lack of focus, accomplishment, or responsibility.

THE NUMBER 4

Positive aspects: Self-discipline; physical and emotional strength; determination; practicality; hard physical worker; concentration; order; focus; appreciation of rules, regulations, and routine.

Negative aspects: Lack of self-discipline (or overdisciplined); all work and no play; too practical; too cautious; stingy; stubborn; lost in drudgery; inability to see big picture.

THE NUMBER 5

Positive aspects: Expansion; change; sensuality; sexuality; freedom; passion; adventure; high energy; activity; curiosity; new opportunities; open to others; highly charismatic.

Negative aspects: Lack of discipline; overindulgence; addictions; impulsive; restless; fickle; rebellious; off center; sensual indulgence.

THE NUMBER 6

Positive aspects: Social consciousness; family and group responsibility; fairness; creator of group harmony; therapist; healer; clairvoyant; teacher of truth and justice; community, home, and family focused.

Negative aspects: Social irresponsibility; meddling in the affairs of others; slave to others' needs; overanxious about social problems; self-righteous; obstinate in world opinions; supercritical of loved ones.

THE NUMBER 7

Positive aspects: Intellectual and spiritual focus; scientific; wise; dignified; refined; sensitive; perfectionist; psychically aware; metaphysical; philosophical; secretive; needs to be alone; studious; bridging gaps between physical and metaphysical; loves mental analysis; acquires by attraction rather than force; is taking a sabbatical from physical world for study.

Negative aspects: Isolated; hypersensitive; withdrawing; skeptical; melancholic; aloof; sarcastic; escapes into drugs or alcohol; seeks perfection in material world rather than in higher knowledge.

THE NUMBER 8

Positive aspects: Material accomplishment; wealth; power; generosity; career accomplishment; business success; high finance; profitable; executive; authoritative; philanthropist.

Negative aspects: Greed; abuse of power; manipulative; selfishness; bully; cruel; braggart; superficial; materialistic; controlling; stingy.

THE NUMBER 9

Positive aspects: Humanitarian; selfless service; universal awareness and understanding; compassion for all people; tolerant; generous; accomplished artist or thinker; impersonal; fair; fulfilled; wise; able to let go; highly charismatic.

Negative aspects: Bitterness; sadness; focused on past and loss; sorrowful; selfish; unconcerned about universal conditions such as global warming; extravagant; blames others; wasteful; unable to move forward; uses charisma for wrong purposes.

THE MASTER NUMBER 11

Positive aspects: Idealistic; refined; visionary; intuitive; artistic; highest plane of intellectual and spiritual advancement; avant-garde; sees both sides; androgynous; humanitarian.

Negative aspects: Fanatic; delusions of grandeur; egocentricity; dishonesty; perverted; too easily wounded by others; sees greatness only in self, not those around him or her.

THE MASTER NUMBER 22

Positive aspects: Practical idealism; uses inspired vision for everyday problems; practical genius; creator of the future; master of the material to benefit all humanity; philanthropist; attracts power on every level; international accomplishment; highest form of service to mankind.

Negative aspects: Material greed; get-rich-quick; abuse of power; indifference to suffering; lost in hard work.

YOUR UNIQUE DESTINY PLAN—YOUR BIRTH-PATH NUMBER

Here's a step-by-step guide to figuring out your birth-path number and what that means about your career choices. We're focusing only on your career path, which is where you've chosen to express your gifts and talents—to make the world a better place in your unique way.

In the calculations below, reduce all numbers down to a single digit—except for the master numbers 22 and 11.

For example, if you were finding the destiny path for someone whose birthday was September 15, 1951, you would do this:

September = 9
15 = 6 (1 + 5 = 6)
1951 = 7 (1 + 9 + 5 + 1 = 16) (1 + 6 = 7)

Total: 22 (9 month + 6 day + 7 year = 22 master number)

This calculation reveals a 22 master birth path—meaning that this person has the great potential of a 22. As master souls, 22s have chosen to come here to help change the way we live and work. Yet they also have the day-to-day vibration of a hardworking 4. Their challenge will be to live up to the power and inspired brilliance of a 22 while not getting lost in the drudgery and hard work of a 4. Their gift will be to bring inspiration and enlightenment to everyday practical-life challenges. This mission will be the focus of their highest work.

By the way, this is my birthday. Like many on this path, I spent years lost in the drudgery of the hardworking 4, as a mountaineering instructor, journalist and magazine editor, before stepping up to my big work. I went through several career transitions to get ready for the work I do today.

Calculate your birth-path number here:

Your birth month:
Your birth date:
Your birth year:

Total:

....

Reduced to a single digit:
(Remember, 10 equals 1 (1 + 0 = 1).)

Your birth-path or destined-work number:

Let's explore exactly what that number means about your career path.

BIRTH-PATH NUMBER I
You can't blend in and get lost in the group. Yours is the destiny of the leader; you must imagine new things, introduce new concepts, delegate the details. People will happily line up behind your unique voice. Don't let ego and criticism blind you to the gifts of your loved

ones, or you'll end up alone. Nurture the best in others with your powerful leadership. For example, you'd be fulfilling your destiny as a cutting-edge designer, editor, consultant, teacher, speaker, author, director, or inventor. Others with your path include Nicolas Cage, Truman Capote, George Clooney, Danny DeVito, Walt Disney, Sally Field, Tom Hanks, Anne Heche, Hulk Hogan, Holly Hunter, Scarlett Johansson, Janis Joplin, Larry King, Martin Luther King, Jr., Carl Sagan, Sting, Barbara Walters, Kate Winslet.

BIRTH-PATH NUMBER 2

You must work in cooperation with others. You're a great team player or family member who is happy working in government or large corporations. You'll be a tower of compassion and support to those for whom you're responsible. You'll be great with details, known for your kindness and sensitivity. Beware the pitfalls of hypersensitivity; cultivate a thicker skin to be successful; and don't get lost in the details. Examples: public relations executive, secretary, administrative assistant, band musician, researcher for a pharmaceutical company or publishing house, life coach, counselor, or hypnotherapist. Others include Jennifer Aniston, Orlando Bloom, Meg Ryan, Gene Simmons, Emma Watson, Frank Lloyd Wright.

MASTER BIRTH-PATH NUMBER 11

You have star quality and creative genius and are capable of the highest forms of artistic creation and inspired ideas. You can potentially change the consciousness of humanity with your artistic gifts—when you use them to help others. You'll attract great praise and criticism as you live up to your brilliant path. Be wary of going off on tangents, or being oversensitive, and strive to maintain balance, or you won't accomplish everything you came to do. Examples: artist, filmmaker, political reformer, diplomat, psychic, mystic, writer, philosopher, musician. Others include Prince Charles, Bill Clinton, John Glenn, Katharine Hepburn, Barack Obama, Jacqueline Kennedy Onassis, John McCain, Paul Simon.

BIRTH-PATH NUMBER 3

Social grace, playfulness, and beauty are your expressions; you love being onstage or in front of a camera or classroom. Your work must involve creative self-expression and leading others (as a teacher or writer) to find their unique ways to express themselves. Words and ideas are key to your self-expression. Don't get too stuck in your cerebral viewpoint or you'll lose the way. Be wary of expecting to be provided for and becoming a financial burden to loved ones. Your gifts of creativity and teaching should provide a fine living. Examples: actor, singer, talk-show host, freelance journalist, interior designer, dancer, beautician, fashion model, hostess, social director, elementary school teacher, arts therapist. Others include Hillary Clinton, Salvador Dalí, Jennifer Lopez, Madonna, Winona Ryder, Gloria Vanderbilt.

BIRTH-PATH NUMBER 4

Practicality, self-discipline, strength, and determination are your gifts. No matter what, you'll get it done. You're the workhorse who develops efficiency systems with your logical mind and great ability to concentrate; you pare things down to their essential nature. The details of building complex structures come easily to you, so you're needed to help launch every great project. Don't get lost in the details, however, or your hard work won't be as productive. Examples: accountant, software technician, mathematician, engineer, draftsman, mechanic, ecologist, general contractor, professional athlete, electrician, economist, chiropractor, newspaper journalist. Others include Pamela Anderson, Julius Caesar, Leonardo da Vinci, Will Smith, Hilary Swank.

MASTER BIRTH-PATH NUMBER 22

You're destined for unparalleled material power and success from making significant, inspired contributions to the way we think and live our everyday lives through business, politics, art, or the humanities. Your work is to guide the less enlightened into a brighter future and teach the most enlightened new principles of forward thinking. Always think big and seek out leaders who will open their doors to you. Your salvation lies in seeing the big picture, following your inspiration, and not getting lost in details, drudgery, or routine. Examples: political organizer, architect, public reformer, benefactor, mass media executive, CEO of innovative corporation, film director, author. Others include Clint Eastwood, Henry Ford, Hugh Hefner, Linda McCartney, Paul McCartney, Mike Nichols, Brad Pitt, Arnold Schwarzenegger, M. Night Shyamalan, Oprah Winfrey.

BIRTH-PATH NUMBER 5

Yours is the path of the charismatic adventurer, sensual explorer, freedom seeker, and agent of change. You're not suited for routine or convention. Expansion and fearlessness are your key values. Change is your most powerful ally and guides you through life. You're a natural salesperson or advertising executive who lives on the road. Marketing and promotion are easy for you, and you'll thrive with travel, fashion, food, and entertainment careers. Yet you need meaning and purpose to anchor you, or life will get too chaotic. Examples: sales, advertising, publicist, foodie, wine connoisseur, travel writer, life coach, actor, professional mountaineering guide, international fashion model, travel-show host, international language teacher. Others include Marlon Brando, Ron Howard, Angelina Jolie, Rudolf Nureyev, Isabella Rossellini, Uma Thurman, Lana Turner, Catherine Zeta-Jones.

BIRTH-PATH NUMBER 6

You have global consciousness, and you're drawn to work for justice and social order. You'll bring harmony and enlightenment to communities as an educator, politician, therapist, doctor, intuitive counselor, or judge. The medical profession, social work, politics, and education are all good fits. You may also be drawn to the arts, but as a producer or director responsible for the group. Home and family are essential to your happiness. Be wary of obsessing on the needs of the group and ignoring your own, which leads to frustration and lack of fulfillment. Examples: teacher, social worker, therapist, doctor, nurse, civil servant, counselor, parent, cook, choreographer, film director. Others include Hank Aaron, Ben Affleck, George Balanchine, Humphrey Bogart, John Denver, John Lennon, Lindsay Lohan, Christopher Reeve, Meryl Streep.

BIRTH-PATH NUMBER 7

Your path is mental reflection and internal analysis—studying the higher meaning of life rather than aggressively pursuing success through the world of business. Powerful intuition, refinement, science, and philosophy are your destinies in this lifetime of study. You'll eventually translate that higher knowledge for the masses as a teacher, writer, actor, or designer. The spiritual and mystical call you, and therein lies your ultimate fulfillment. You'll be happiest working alone in your highly refined destiny. Examples: scientist, psychiatrist, psychologist, minister, doctor of divinity, researcher, investigator, science or mystery writer, philosopher, artist, or designer. Others include Paula Abdul, Christian Bale, Leonard Bernstein, Johnny Depp, Hugh Grant, George Harrison, Al Pacino, Julia Roberts, Andy Warhol.

BIRTH-PATH NUMBER 8

Financial success, big business, entrepreneurship, or professional athlete are all on your destined path. You won't work for minimum wage very long before you become the CEO of the company. You'll quickly be pulled to the top, where you'll be recognized for your executive leadership. Power and wealth are your destiny and challenge as you learn to use your power for good in the world. Think big, launch your own company, and avoid power-abuse pitfalls. Overcome greediness by developing compassion and generosity of spirit. Use your abundance to fund the causes you care about. Examples: manufacturer, CEO, banker, entrepreneur, stockbroker, retail owner, financier, professional athlete, supermodel, publisher, political official. Others include Muhammad Ali, Lucille Ball, Joan Crawford, Matt Damon, Jane Fonda, Stanley Kubrick, Paul Newman, Pablo Picasso, Martha Stewart, Shannon Tweed, Tennessee Williams.

BIRTH-PATH NUMBER 9

Inspiring others with your compassion for the human condition and deep understanding of universal truths, you'll work with several foundations and schools—as you continually let go of what you've finished and move forward gracefully. Your free spirit, broad knowledge, wisdom, and compassion will make you highly charismatic. Your work will be humanitarian, service oriented, and artistically inclined. Mysticism will intrigue you. Don't get lost in bitterness and disappointment from looking back at the past. Reach out to the unknown future. Examples: publisher, lecturer, composer, playwright, physician, humanitarian, political leader, international physician, author, philanthropist, founder of nonprofit foundations. Others include

Jimmy Carter, Harrison Ford, Jimi Hendrix, Whitney Houston, Charles Lindbergh, Shirley MacLaine, Yoko Ono, Elvis Presley, Robert Redford, James Van Pragh.

TO SUMMARIZE THIS CHAPTER

◆ Pythagoras saw that everything in the universe operated in predictable cycles, and his basic units of measuring each cycle were the digits 1 through 9.

◆ According to Pythagoras each number has a meaning or vibration, and by adding the numbers within your birthday and reducing them to single digits, you reveal the nature of the work you came here to do.

◆ To find your birth-path number, add the digits of your birth date, month, and year and reduce them down to a single digit (or master number 11 or 22).

For example, for the birth date October 16, 1980, do this:
Month = October equals 10, equals 1
1 = (1 + 0)
Date = 16, equals 7
7 = (1 + 6)
Year = 1980, equals 9
9 = (1 + 9 + 8 + 0 = 18), (1 + 8)

Total of month (1) plus date (7) plus year (9) equals 17, equals 8
8 = (1 + 7)
Birth path = 8

Do yours:
Your birth month:
Your birth date:
Your birth year:

Total:

Reduced down to a single digit:
(Remember, 10 = 1 + 0 = 1.)

Your birth-path or destined-work number:

8

PERILS AND POTENTIALS OF A GREAT PATH

Insights for Those on the Path of 11 or 22

IMAGINE THAT YOU'RE HANGING out on the other side about to jump back in for another adventure on planet Earth. You've already experienced several rounds of lifetimes mastering the lessons everyone struggles with: independence, relationships, hard work, adventure, sensuality, spirituality, higher learning, use of power, selflessness, and humanitarianism. You've graduated!

Now you're being asked to go back in to provide guidance for others as a master soul on the path of 11 or 22. "I'm not sure," you say. "What if I fall off path and forget my mission?"

"Well, you probably will at some point," explain your guides. "Most master souls forget when they go back. They get lost in the negativity of human experience and don't understand why their perspective on life is so different from everyone else's. They waste time thinking they're inadequate or inferior. But eventually they remember and get it done."

You turn to me standing beside you. "Are you going to go back on a master path too?"

"I'm studying for it, preparing. But I'm pretty worried," I admit. "It won't be easy."

We discuss it for quite awhile, and still you're not convinced until one of your old soul mates stops by for a visit.

"I'll make an agreement," she whispers to you. "If you go back in, I'll be your lover or your child. I'll remind you of what you came to do. And you can help me remember my mission. Will you agree to that?" she asks you.

I can feel the tremendously deep, lifetimes-old love between the two of you. I bask in the energy running between you. You look into her eyes. "Okay. I'll do it. I agree," is all you say, never taking your eyes away from hers.

"We'll remember, right?" you whisper to her.

"Yes, whenever you look into my eyes, you'll remember," she says.

You sign up for the master path lifetime—knowing that your soul mates will help you find your way and remember who you are.

Yet it's a daunting challenge. Because the moment we're born into the human realm, the process of forgetting who we are begins. Family, friends, and cultural belief systems all lovingly provide misguidance about the purpose of a lifetime.

From early on we hear:

"Who do you think you are to . . . ?"

"Do you really think you're good enough to . . . ?"

"Why can't you be like everybody else?"

"Smart people only do such and such for a living."

Our peers and family judge us by how well we fit in and behave like them. These conventional messages push everyone off path. But they're especially crippling for the master soul who has come in to be different, stand out, and make a difference in a bold way.

The 11 and 22 master path souls have powerful feelings, passions, sensitivities, and ideas that they struggle to fit into mainstream ways of living. Their lives are more intense and dramatic than other people's.

They usually reach a point when they choose to follow the path of least resistance by fitting in and playing it small. Eventually they step up to the work they've signed up for—which takes courage and wisdom.

These choice points often come during what's known in astrology as our two Saturn returnings. These life-changing events occur around the ages of twenty-nine and fifty-eight. But smaller reinvention opportunities occur several times during the lifetime—whenever we go through a nine-year transition. (See chapter 10 for more explanation of the nine-year transition.)

If you're on the 11/2 path your particular gift of heightened sensitivity will also be your challenge. Extreme intuition will make you a gifted artist or healer, yet you'll doubt yourself. You'll see early on that you're different from others and don't fit in. You'll have to decide if that's going to stop you from your mission, or if you can look to your higher guidance and find inspiration to keep moving forward. Having a strong spiritual belief system, whatever way you define that, will definitely help you.

Many people in your life will disappoint you. It's hard living up to the heightened sensitivities, gifts, and visions of the 11/2 path. You'll be told you're too high strung and that you need to dial it down. It would be best to stay close to other master souls—those on higher vibrational frequencies—if you can find them. Be careful whom you share your affections with and how well equipped they are to meet your expectations—which are great. You'll find inner peace and fulfillment when you look to your highest self and spiritual guidance for wisdom, then share that wisdom with others as a teacher-healer.

If you're on the 22/4 path your pitfalls and potentials are different from the 11/2. You'll be drawn to hard work, organizing, building, strengthening, and promoting healthy lifestyles. Your downfall could be getting lost in the details of drudgery work. I've met several 22/4 path people who were engineers or architects wanting to build innovative systems and structures for the world, but they got detoured by the drudgery and tediousness of everyday work life. They didn't step up to their great work until they had a health crisis—a soul awakening—that reminded them of their greater mission.

If 22/4 is your path be sure that your work is in alignment with this mission: to bring inspired new ideas and innovative solutions to help others; to change the way people live their everyday lives. Your work must involve new thought, alternative ideas, courage, and boldness.

I've studied many people on the 22 path—friends, clients, and celebrities. It's been fascinating to watch their lives unfold. For example, Brad Pitt navigated his soul turning point by funding world organizations to fight poverty in third-world countries, creating energy-efficient housing projects for low-income Katrina survivors in New Orleans, and funding political movements that encourage people to live up to their potential. He became a true visionary and philanthropist—fostering new ideas that help the world move forward.

Oprah is also on the 22/4 path. She launched her career as a hard-working journalist and eventually became a media mogul promoting some of the most inspiring and life-changing programs ever offered on mainstream television (such as her series with Eckhart Tolle). She presents ideas that change the way we live our lives. That's a perfect example of the 22/4 mission.

Film director M. Night Shyamalan is also on a 22/4 path. His two most successful films (*Sixth Sense* and *Signs*) helped raise consciousness by offering new ideas for our consideration. Whether he was showing how and why spirits need help crossing over to the other dimension (in *Sixth Sense*) or revealing the divine order always evident in our lives (in *Signs*), those two films left people contemplating new ideas about how the world works.

When people on the 22/4 path listen to conventional advice about the direction their work should take, they can get quite lost. They may dumb down their work to fit into the hardworking drudgery vibration of the number 4 until they're exhausted and adrift. Yet they know they came here to do something meaningful, and they don't understand why other people are content with meaningless work.

Fitting in is never the right course of action for the 22/4 or the 11/2.

On my journey as a 22/4 growing up in the South during the fifties, I was ashamed of how different my thoughts and beliefs were from those around me. I felt like an alien who had landed in a strange world. Yet I was told by teachers, family, and friends to be like everybody else. So I shut down and didn't speak my truth or acknowledge what my intuition revealed.

I turned away from my higher guidance and made choices that were not in alignment with my true self or what I came to do. The self-doubt, loneliness, and depression that plagued my early years is very typical of someone on the 22/4 path. I didn't want to disappoint my well-educated and conventional-thinking family, so I worked hard in careers that didn't fit.

During a nine-year reinvention point I came out of the closet as an intuitive and began to live up to my potential, helping others remember their life mission and manifest it through career. I released my need for acceptance, embraced my true gifts, and surrendered the outcome. As divine order states, when we live and work true to our mission, success follows. So it has in my life.

If you're on a master path but feeling lost, please meditate or pray at least twenty minutes a day to quiet the chatter in your mind and tap into your higher guidance. That alone can save your life and remind you of your greater mission.

If you feel that you must be on a master path but your birth date only adds up to a 2 or a 4, try adding it two different ways and see what you come up with. In traditional numerology books, you'll find only one acceptable way of adding up your date of birth and coming up with the master numbers 11 or 22. For example:

> September 15, 1951, is my birth date. Traditionally my path is calculated this way:

September = 9
15 = 6 (1 + 5)
1951 = 7 (1 + 9 + 5 + 1 = 16 = 1 + 6)
9 + 6 + 7 = 22

However, there's another way to add up this birth date:

$$
\begin{array}{r}
1951 \\
15 \\
+9 \\
\hline
1975
\end{array}
$$

1975 = 1 + 9 + 7 + 5 = 22

As you can see, both ways of adding this birth date equal 22. When a birth date adds up to a master path number of 11 or 22, whichever way you add it (as shown above), it means these souls chose to have a lifetime that gave no way out of their mission. They didn't want the ability to get lost in conventional ways of living. Their vibration would make it almost impossible for them to fit in and succeed at ordinary work. They would be viewed as "different" by the world.

If, however, your birth date adds up to a master path number of 11 or 22 only by adding it *one* of the ways illustrated above, it shows you've given yourself a choice within the lifetime. You'll be able to fit in with more ease, and you'll succeed at more conventional work. However, you'll hit a turning point—a soul reinvention point—when you'll be required to step up to your master path mission.

For example, August 1, 1955, equals a 2 path when you add it this way:

1955
   8
+1
___
1964 = 20 = 2
(1 + 9 + 6 + 4 = 20 = 2 + 0 = 2)

But if you add it this way, it equals the master path 11:
1955 = 2 (1 + 9 + 5 + 5 = 20 = 2 + 0 = 2)
   8
+1
___
  11

Having this choice can be a blessing and a curse. When it's easy to fit in and get by, it becomes harder to wake yourself up to do your great work. While your lifetime may be smoother and look more normal from the outside, you risk never waking up and getting to your important work. Yet the deep unrest in your soul will gnaw at you to do something important eventually—as was the case of my client Joseph in chapter 6.

If you're on the path of 11 or 22, be sure to add your birth date both ways and see what you get and what you can learn from that. It can be very helpful information during your reinvention points.

Here's another way to see if you have a hidden 11 or 22 path number. If you find that you're on the 11 or 22 path by adding your birth date this way, it means that you've given yourself a choice within the lifetime about when and if you'll live up to your great work as a master soul. When you're ready to do the work, it may seem that you've appeared out of nowhere to get it done.

President Barack Obama's 11 master path number is hidden in this way. For example: his birth date is August 4, 1961. When you add his birth date the traditional way, it appears he's on the path of the number 2. However, add his birth date this way:

$$8 + 4 + 1 + 9 + 6 + 1 = 29 = 2 + 9 = 11$$

Now you see his hidden 11 master soul path. See if your birth date adds up to a master soul path by adding it this way.

TO SUMMARIZE THIS CHAPTER

◆ If your birth date digits down to an 11/2 birth path, it means you're on the path of a master soul. You have star quality, creative and intuitive genius, and are capable of the highest forms of artistic creation and healing work.

◆ If your birth date digits down to a 22/4 birth path, it means you're a master soul who is here to make significant contributions that reshape the course of thought, industry, politics, art, or humanities.

◆ If you're a master path soul on the 11/2 path, you'll need to learn to use your heightened sensitivity to inspire through beauty and the arts, to heal others, and not to be wounded by criticism.

◆ If you're a master soul on the 22/4 path, be careful not to lose yourself in hard work and drudgery. Yes, you're incredibly strong. Use that strength to focus on the big ideas of life and help change the way we live our everyday lives. Don't spend your life doing hard work for hard work's sake.

◆ If you're a master soul, add your birth date two different ways, as described in this chapter. This reveals whether your master path involves a choice point for stepping up to your great work or if your vibration will make it difficult to fit in from early on.

9

THE FLAVOR OF YOUR WORK

I F YOU'RE ON A 7 birth path and your sister is too, why do you navigate your lives so differently? One answer lies in your astrological sun sign. Perhaps she's a Taurus and you're a Pisces. If so, she will be slow to act, very grounded and practical in her mission, sometimes stubborn, and always strong. Whereas you'll be intuitive, more inclined to go with the flow, emotional in your responses, and come more often from the right-brain, creative, spiritual point of view, while she comes from the linear, logical, left-brain point of view.

Yet you both have the same mission—because you're both on the 7 birth path.

I'll explain how this works.

You probably already know your astrological sun sign and have been told that it reveals certain traits about you. You may have had a more advanced astrological reading done that included an in-depth analysis of your life challenges and opportunities. How do the numbers in your birth date interface with this astrological interpretation? In many, many ways. I'm going to keep it simple, though, and focus on how your sun sign interacts with and flavors your birth path.

Let's go back to our prelifetime discussions on the other side. We're having tea again, discussing our options for the next lifetime. You've just decided that you're ready to jump back in for another round. Your birth path will be a 7; you'll be drawn to study the higher meaning of life from science to art and spirituality. On this path you'll be very intuitive and have a tendency to isolate yourself.

If you decide to wrap your birth-path number with the Sagittarius sun sign, you'll be naturally outgoing, gregarious, and easily get along with others. This will help keep you from isolating too much or being too sensitive. Yet it could also pull you off path; You may spend your early years partying with friends rather than following your higher mission.

But if you wrap the 7 birth path with Pisces, your intuition and feelings will be supertuned and force you to look beyond the seen world for guidance—probably from a very young age. That's a good thing for accomplishing your mission, unless you get lost in that hypersensitivity, lose your confidence, and find yourself unable to fit in to the world to make a living.

If you decide to wrap your 7 path with Virgo, well, that's a whole other flavor. You'll be pulled out into the world seeking physical perfection with your analytical mind. To live up to your 7 path mission, you'll need to evolve from seeking perfection in the material world to seeking inner perfection. Eventually you'll find spiritual purpose and stop focusing on superficial details.

So let's see what we can learn about your mission by understanding the sun sign flavor you wrapped around your birth-path number. All you need to know is your birth date for this, not the time of birth or location. Here's a brief overview of the sun signs and their flavors.

ARIES (RAM) = MARCH 21–APRIL 19

If you wrapped your birth-path number with Aries, you will be powerful and bold—leading others to new ideas. Yours is not a lifetime for retreating to a mountaintop to reflect on the higher meanings of life. You'll be at the forefront of all endeavors, be they business, sports, or humanitarian work. This flavor is not for the meek, and if you chose it, live up to it. But remember that your great work is about empowering others—not overpowering them.

ARIES 1 PATH: Born to lead and take no prisoners; you'll keep moving forward with unique visions and ideas, following your authentic voice until others take notice. Powerful and bold, you'll make your mark as a CEO, leadership coach, teacher, or performer. Just remember the higher mission is to lead and inspire others rather than go it alone, focusing only on your needs.

ARIES 2 PATH: As a couples therapist or music teacher, you'll help and support others, which is your ultimate mission. But you'll probably start out drawn to the more mundane details of life, whether it's software, administrative assistance, or accounting. Your home will be impeccable, yet your challenge is to look up from those mundane details and bring healing and intuitive wisdom to those around you.

ARIES 3 PATH: As an entertainer you can delight and uplift others from any stage. You'll have great ideas, brilliant creativity, and the ability to dazzle—whether you're a chef, interior designer, high school teacher, or fiction writer. As a teacher or politician, you'll lead people to new heights of knowledge and inspiration. Don't play too much in your early years or rely on others for financial support; you're very capable of making good money from your trade.

ARIES 4 PATH: There's so much strength and bright mental energy in this path that you'll never have any trouble getting a job. You'll work hard wherever you land and soon become a manager. The problem will be choosing a job that lets your intellect shine through and gives you the opportunity to lead. Remember, you're a builder of systems and structures, but you're also here to lead others, not just toil away in the drudgery. Follow your gut and step out front as a teacher, manager, or leader; you'll thrive.

ARIES 5 PATH: You're destined to teach and write about the fearless adventures that feed your soul—such as mountaineering or skydiving. Don't settle down. Instead, take others with you on far-flung travels and make money as a guide or travel writer. Find your center, but venture out constantly on exotic journeys. Teach that passionate living to others, even as a language teacher who inspires people to expand their worlds.

ARIES 6 PATH: At first you may lose your path as you cater to others, but soon you'll own up to your gifts of healing. You may choose alternative means of healing such as acupuncture, or you may take the role of family therapist. Either way you'll ultimately end up teaching what you know to others—but not in a conventional classroom. When you finally sit in the chair of the healer, you'll recognize your full power and be able to use your intuitive gifts to help others.

ARIES 7 PATH: You would do well writing screenplays for Hollywood or becoming a world-renowned graphic designer. Your brilliant mind, ability to learn anything—from psychology and science to art—and your natural talent at writing will give you many choices. But whatever you do, it will have to be cutting-edge work or you'll get bored. Be prepared to have others look to you for inspiration.

ARIES 8 PATH: Power and force will be your opportunities and lessons. You must always be in charge; yet becoming the benevolent leader is your challenge. You'll attract great success and wealth and eventually learn to temper your controlling behavior in relationships. Your ultimate work uses power generously to change the world; you'll start companies that sell products and services that uplift and inspire.

ARIES 9 PATH: The world needs you to lead us beyond the limits of our understanding, whether you're a university physics teacher, minister, humanitarian worker in a third-world country, or an inspired musician. Teach, write, and start your own nonprofit foundation.

ARIES 11 PATH: This is a lofty mission—one that puts you out in front of large numbers of people. Whether you choose to change our world through politics, education, or the arts, you won't do it quietly. Strengthen your core so that criticism doesn't wipe you out, and you'll be relaxed at the podium, which is where you belong.

ARIES 22 PATH: Stand up tall—because you're here to be in front of people. Your bold ideas will change lives, whether you choose politics, health, or education. This path of inspired leadership transcends mere humanitarianism and takes you on a journey of transforming the way the world behaves—and always from the stage.

TAURUS (BULL) = APRIL 20–MAY 20

If Taurus is the flavor you chose, you're made of pure force and solid willpower. You love feeling the ground beneath your feet. Being practical puts you at ease. You may take awhile to get going on your higher mission, but once the bull is moving, look out! Its strength is unstoppable. Yet the bull always retains its connection to the earth and its practical sensibilities. So even if your mission is to be a great humanitarian or spiritual teacher, Taurus energy will keep it real.

TAURUS 1 PATH: You'll enjoy a happy life of personal power, charisma, leadership skills, and pure physicality. You could be a great quarterback, fashion model, or general contractor. But remember to open your heart to others and develop compassion. Loosen your grip on practical reality enough to see the higher purpose of things.

TAURUS 2 PATH: At your best you're strong, yet sensitive and supportive. At your worst you're stubborn and too focused on mundane details. Rise to your full potential and use your gifts of sensitivity and strength (a rare combination) to heal relationships or teach others to make fine detailed furniture, brilliant gardens, and exquisite pottery. If you focus completely on the details of computer software, it will make you crazy. Focus on people as often as things.

TAURUS 3 PATH: The world is your canvas—create with your hands making things that delight us with beauty and originality. Whether you're cooking, creating art, building homes, or teaching us how to do those things, your bright touch will make your creations unique and practical. Use your hands, keep it real, and you'll make a fine living.

TAURUS 4 PATH: This is the path of the powerful, practical, hardworking, get-it-all-done builder of systems and foundations. If that sounds like a lot of work, it is. Without you there would be no practical, physical structure to our lives. You organize us, build our homes and highways, and run our hospitals. Along the way enjoy your physical strength to swing a bat or lift weights. We depend on your practical hardworking gifts to keep our world running—whether you choose engineering, nursing, construction, administrative work, or being a COO.

TAURUS 5 PATH: Your urge to travel and live life passionately is tempered by your need to stay grounded and practical. Yet your mission is to expand and not constrict. Be unconventional in order to find your happiness—whether that means teaching people to ski or make pottery or being a life or sports coach. Don't give away your joy to fit in.

TAURUS 6 PATH: As a dancer and artist, you'll dazzle us with your visions. But later you may decide to become a chiropractor or medical technician. Serving others will soothe your soul, and you can bring your artistic talent along with you as a dance or art therapist.

TAURUS 7 PATH: Study psychology, astronomy, physics, geology, biology, and spirituality—as you embrace the higher meaning of life. You'll be a great science writer, and your photography will capture the essence of things. Ultimately you'll teach others your advanced knowledge.

TAURUS 8 PATH: With power and practicality as driving forces, you probably won't search for higher meaning until you hit your Saturn returnings at ages twenty-nine and fifty-eight. At those major turning points you may find yourself calling a career intuitive who will advise you (correctly) to start your own business creating and selling practical, everyday products—which will reap great financial rewards for you.

TAURUS 9 PATH: There's something of a struggle here as you try to balance your fascination with the divine mysteries and your down-to-earth practicality. On one hand you may not even believe in miracles. Yet you have precognitive dreams that come true and hear other people's thoughts. With one foot firmly on the ground and the other in the ethers, your challenge is to shake loose the foot that's planted too firmly on terra firma and manifest your great humanitarian mission of teaching and spiritual service. You could be an alternative healer or an emergency room technician. Ultimately, being a spiritual teacher/writer will set your spirit free.

TAURUS 11 PATH: With extreme sensitivity, highly developed intuition, and an intense grip on reality, your work will be an elegant combination of the profound and mundane, teaching and healing in the most practical of ways. You'll be drawn to gardening, piano, and pottery. Ultimately you'll work as a therapist who helps people survive in crisis situations.

TAURUS 22 PATH: It may take you awhile (a couple of major life reinventions) before you own up to your 22 work and stop focusing on the drudgery of working for work's sake. You can be stubborn and too focused on the practical. But in your fifties you'll get to the great work and make a difference in people's day-to-day lives—whether you choose the medical field or community politics.

GEMINI (TWINS) = MAY 21–JUNE 21

Your agile, hungry mind is a great gift, but it can distract you from the intuitive knowledge of what's right for your life. You'll change perspectives frequently, study every situation from several viewpoints, and become quite brilliant, cunning, and accomplished. But let your heart and intuition serve as your compass, or you'll lose your way and fall far off path.

GEMINI 1 PATH: You're the brilliant leader with endless new ideas. Focus on the path ahead, make decisions; lead and teach your ideas, your way. Creativity and vision are your trademarks. As a CEO, political strategist, school principal, or author of educational reform books and policies, you'll fulfill your mission.

GEMINI 2 PATH: Everything in your journey comes in twos—especially your dual nature. You're smart, cunning, and manipulative, but, at your best, you use those traits to support others to do their great work. When not living up to your potential, that small-minded yet brilliant focus on the mundane details of accounting, software, or marketing will make you (and those around you) crazy. Use your brilliance instead as a teacher of great ideas, a public relations genius, or to develop nursing software that prevents medication mistakes and improves hospital safety standards.

GEMINI 3 PATH: Could there be anyone as brilliant or creative as you are? This is a path of the brightest mind—here to write, teach, and uplift us with creative energy and new thoughts. Find your spiritual center so you don't get lost in the world of never-ending ideas. Use your mind to make a huge difference in business and education—whether you choose classroom teaching or political reform.

GEMINI 4 PATH: When we need someone to solve our transportation problems or develop a new form of natural energy, we'll turn to you. Your enlightened new engineering systems and solutions can change the world. And don't ignore your gifts as a journalist. Whether you choose print or broadcast, you'll be the smartest, hardest-working reporter in your field.

GEMINI 5 PATH: This is a powerful combination of beauty, brains, and charisma. You can't be tied down easily. If you commit to someone you'll probably have affairs—until you find your purpose in life. But this beauty, brains, and charisma formula is on purpose: Use it to make a difference in the global condition by calling our attention to problems that need solving. When everyone wants to look at you, it's your responsibility to stand alongside of the issues that matter. As an actor, company spokesperson, or documentary film producer, use your power wisely.

GEMINI 6 PATH: The world needs doctors (both alternative and conventional) like you. You're here to find the cure no one else could find or to teach young doctors how to find it. Even if you start out in the business world, teaching companies how to make profits, ultimately you'll own up to your gifts and redirect your life, choosing to be a therapist, medical researcher, or naturopathic physician.

GEMINI 7 PATH: This is a wicked-smart combination: Go to graduate school so you can use your intelligence to inspire and educate those who need it most. (Don't choose law school, or you'll be disappointed by the lack of ethics in day-to-day practice.) Your philosophical books and spiritual essays will be admired for years to come.

GEMINI 8 PATH: Your mission is to own your power in the world of finance and business, and to show others a brighter way of navigating enterprise. With your head full of innovative ideas, you'll start several businesses and sell products such as software and books that help solve our educational and economic woes. Don't answer to anyone else or give your power away to partners. Lead your own company to greatness.

GEMINI 9 PATH: You could be the genius who invents a solution to worldwide poverty and disease—as long as you don't get stuck in bitterness about the past. Focus on our global future, not just your future, and you'll be successful. Move into a position of power and influence where your ideas will be heard and you can inspire action, such as politics, nonprofit foundations, educating the educators, and leading global initiatives. If that feels too big, start out by becoming an educator or journalist, and let the path unfold before you.

GEMINI 11 PATH: I hope you'll pursue music lessons as a child and later compose concertos that heal our hearts and minds. We'll also be content if you write books that inspire or teach young scientists how to think. Your mission is big; careers in the arts or education will help you live up to it. Don't worry about the opinions of others, and move forward fearlessly.

GEMINI 22 PATH: Use your visionary mind to create new systems for the world that improve our everyday lives. Careers in law, medicine, and politics await you. Start by getting a teaching certificate or Ph.D. so you can teach what you know. Meditate daily to keep from changing directions too often. Focus on the highest ideals, and empower the masses rather than manipulate those less intelligent than you.

CANCER (CRAB) = JUNE 22–JULY 22

Your heightened sensitivity and secretive nature are at once your gift and your challenge. You feel everything and process it through your silent filter rather than readily share it with others. Yet your feelings and intuitions are your gift. Don't hide that brilliant wisdom and insight and retreat into a hole of self-doubt and fear. Show your sensitivity to the world, bare your sweet soul, and speak the truth.

CANCER 1 PATH: The crab must come out of its shell to lead others; you'll have to emerge into your power slowly at first. But you will— once you stop retreating. Don't let sensitivity hold you back. At your best you'll lead groups, families, and communities to enlightened ways of living together. You'll be an inspiration as a civic leader, or the CEO of a company that builds cohousing communities.

CANCER 2 PATH: This is a path of pure sensitivity, intuition, and the ability to connect with others. Find your spiritual strength so you're not thrown off balance by those intense emotions. You know what others are thinking. Use that awareness to heal, teach, and help. You may ground yourself in the detailed work of nursing, public relations writing, or keeping executives organized, but your greatest mission is to be an intuitive therapist or healer.

CANCER 3 PATH: Your home will be an endless canvas for the colorful designs and inspired fashions that come so easily to you. As an interior designer, a feng shui practitioner, or a home-stager, you will use your uplifting, unique creativity and blossom into a lucrative career. As a chef, cooking instructor, or fashion designer, you'll also tap into your mission. Don't settle for simply decorating your miserable cubicle while slaving away at a meaningless job. Trust your talents and share them with the world—for good money.

CANCER 4 PATH: Building homes or being a general contractor may be your first career choice. But if you keep evolving to your potential, you'll go to architecture or engineering school and learn to design systems and create innovative living spaces. Either way, your determination and hard work combined with intuitive knowing will get you through life's challenges.

CANCER 5 PATH: Enjoy your wild adventures, but always come back home. Use your depth and insight to help and heal others and to teach fearless living. As a coach, speaker, or writer you can share the lessons learned from addiction recovery and healing your marriage. As a high school counselor you can save the lives of young adults who venture too close to the edge.

CANCER 6 PATH: As a sensitive, caring lover, parent, and teacher, you have great talent for creating harmonious homes and communities, and you're highly intuitive. Whether you first choose to sell homeowners insurance or real estate, eventually you'll become a teacher, coach, or counselor.

CANCER 7 PATH: With powerful grace and intelligence, you'll thrive in careers where your feelings and wisdom can guide you. Whether it's writing, teaching biology, or the arts, your depth and intuition will help you connect deeply with others and guide you to success. Stay away from big business, where your sensitivity could be a liability.

CANCER 8 PATH: You'll be drawn to real estate investments, fix-and-flips, and home-staging. But your true fulfillment will be found when you're running a big company that helps people, such as creating products or services that promote health, well-being, or intuition. Don't give away your power in the beginning of your career. When you're finally at the helm of your own enterprise, your true star power will blossom. The result: a seven-figure bank balance that will be a happy surprise and a grand opportunity for generosity to the causes you believe in.

CANCER 9 PATH: When sensitivity gets the best of you, you may focus on the dark side of your journey and hold on to bitterness and blame. But when using your sensitivity to help others, you'll do great humanitarian-based work. Take your focus off of the mundane, and find your purpose as an alternative healer, language teacher, musician, or writer.

CANCER 11 PATH: Your writing or music talents will blossom early, and audiences will love your inspired ideas and enlightened performances. Use your gift to help others by becoming a brilliant music therapist or intuitive healer. Pursue Reiki (energy work), dream work, and cutting-edge techniques that push the boundaries of conventional healing.

CANCER 22 PATH: Whether you focus on alternative energy, new building techniques, or supporting communities and families in crisis, you'll be a respected visionary. Pursue political activism roles that focus on education or health care, where your gifts will make a huge impact.

LEO (LION) = JULY 23–AUGUST 22

The majestic, warm, and kindly lion, Leo rules with generosity of spirit and fiery passion. Your noble and confident presence will dominate any environment you choose to work in. But don't get lost in the "showmanship." Reach deep into your essence for the purpose of this great path—lighting the fire of higher knowledge.

LEO 1 PATH: All power and pride, your dignified presence will open many doors to success. As an actor or athlete you'll command the stage. Your highest mission, however, is to use that presence to bring attention to those in need. When everyone admires you, it's your responsibility to turn that attention to the causes and ideas that make a difference. Start a company that promotes organic farming or solar energy. Better yet, coach teenagers who feel unworthy and help them find their power.

LEO 2 PATH: Your warmth, sincerity, and brilliance will draw people to you. And your intense sensitivity to the needs of others will guide you to your great work. Whether you choose to start a school or to be a marriage therapist, political science teacher, or inspired politician, you have the charisma, kindness, and brains to make a huge difference. Use your life as an example to help people live up to their own greatest potentials.

LEO 3 PATH: Humor, generosity, and creativity are powerful gifts that will get you far on this path. And you'll spend lots of time entertaining us onstage. Your talent for brilliant communication will leave a legacy, whether you make your living as a speaker, actor, comedian, or as a teacher of languages.

LEO 4 PATH: If anyone wants to get something done, they'll turn to you. Your strength and charisma make you a powerful quarterback, dancer, gold-medal weight lifter, or beach volleyball pro. At your best you'll teach math or engineering at the local high school, where you can coach sports or teach dance after school. If you choose to sit behind a desk, it should be in a newsroom, where you'll thrive as a hardworking broadcast or print journalist.

LEO 5 PATH: With your good looks and authentic charm, you could be the next Denzel Washington. Acting, extreme sports, mountain climbing, travel guiding, teaching, and life coaching will all appeal to you. Just don't push those addiction limits beyond the point of no return. Find your spiritual center so you can enjoy exotic adventures and still have a family.

LEO 6 PATH: As a physician you provide a generous healing presence so comforting that your patients will heal from impossible diseases. As a teacher you inspire your students to score the highest test scores because you believe they can. Your stage presence is potent and believable, whether you choose Shakespeare or leading corporate teams to success. Eventually you may own up to your clairvoyant powers and use them to heal.

LEO 7 PATH: Your analytical mind and philosophical nature make you well suited for a Ph.D. in psychology or political science and a life spent teaching in academia. Even better, you might study to be a Unity minister or Science of the Mind practitioner and inspire others with your divine perspective. You'll have to find a way to combine the analytical, critical thinker inside you with your heart's desire to help others. A classroom podium may be the perfect solution.

LEO 8 PATH: Blessed with charisma, brilliance, and generosity of spirit, you have a responsibility to create a business that improves the global condition. Early in life you may be accused of bullying or manipula-tion. Eventually you'll evolve into a benevolent entrepreneur. Whether you choose to sell solar and wind power, manufacture green cars, start an alternative school, or become a financial adviser, your enter-prise should be unique and offer solutions to our most challenging world problems.

LEO 9 PATH: Your gracious personality, big heart, and enormous spirit will make you well loved in business or the arts. You could take the path of award-winning musician or paradigm-shifting architect. You'll thrive in humanitarian efforts that bring new solutions to energy problems, provide housing for third-world countries, or find innova-tive ways to feed hungry children.

LEO 11 PATH: Your leadership will help us achieve our highest human potential—whenever you're ready to step up to the plate. You'll leave a legacy of enlightened, humanitarian ideas, as long as you keep that brave persona shining and protect your sensitive nature from the wounds of criticism. You'll be a powerful change agent in politics, law, medicine, or the arts. Society will benefit from your inspired de-signs, books, and philosophical insights.

LEO 22 PATH: This is the path of ultimate power; be sure to use your gifts to make positive contributions and inspire social changes in our everyday lives. You're the teacher who creates new learning systems; the writer whose novel changes the way we think; and the actor/di-rector whose films leave us hopeful for a better future.

VIRGO (VIRGIN) = AUGUST 23–SEPTEMBER 22

You are the ultimate seeker of truth and understanding, with your re-lentless analysis and pursuit of perfection that are your gift and curse. In any career you'll get to the core of the problem and perceive the essential truth instantly. Your challenge is to refrain from pointing out those flaws and imperfections until you've found solutions. Otherwise the path can be destructive. Yet your brilliant mind holds our highest potential for life-enhancing solutions.

VIRGO 1 PATH: Your great need for independence and authenticity combined with analytical thinking allow you to see imperfections everywhere you go. Your mission is to teach and lead us to those solutions—compassionately—and to see the good in others as well as their flaws. Once you've mastered that, your visionary talents will help the world enormously as a leadership trainer, political reformer, or the CEO of a software company.

VIRGO 2 PATH: Details will delight you, and nobody's desk will be cleaner and more organized than yours. You'll have a tendency to be too sensitive. Remember to come up for air and see the forest. You'll be appreciated as an office assistant or accountant, yet your true mission is to teach others—using your intuitive knowledge of what people need. As a psychiatrist, nurse, physician's assistant, or math teacher, you'll find a great outlet for your gifts.

VIRGO 3 PATH: Creativity and personal charisma are your powerful gifts. Beware of intellectual arrogance or seeing what's wrong with everything before you consider what's right. Communicate your insights through writing, dancing, publishing, and teaching—with compassion. Pursue careers in television, journalism, or education, and you'll be living up to your potential.

VIRGO 4 PATH: When you apply for a job be sure to say that you can do anything, learn everything, and that you'll work ten times harder than anyone else. That may begin to hint at the depth of your ability to master any subject. Journalism is a must for you; you'll tackle a story and never let it go until you've gotten it right. But don't get lost in the drudgery and details without taking time out to see the big picture. At every meeting they'll give you the hardest projects—whether you decide on engineering, writing, or architecture.

VIRGO 5 PATH: Don't let your analytical mind prevent you from experiencing life as deeply and fully as you're meant to. Travel, climb mountains, play music, and beware of addictions. Use your brilliance to create culinary masterpieces and write best-selling memoirs. You may eventually find yourself teaching music, teaching English as a second language, or running a thriving travel business.

VIRGO 6 PATH: You're a gifted diagnostician, so medical school or social work is a great choice for you. If you choose business, become the trainer who stands in front of the boardroom pointing out weaknesses in management so they can be fixed. Don't aim your critical viewpoint at family members; keep it in the office. Ultimately you may use your talents to diagnose and heal as a therapist or acupuncturist.

VIRGO 7 PATH: Perfectionism, when focused on the external world, will only drive you crazy. You may have an "imperfect" loved one who supplies that lesson—which helps you find your true path. Whether you choose law, philosophy, or quantum physics, you'll analyze the deeper meaning of how life works. Eventually you'll find answers and inner peace through spiritual pursuit. Once you understand the great mysteries, teach and write what you know.

VIRGO 8 PATH: Your brilliant mind will guide you to the enterprise that suits you best—whether it's landscape architecture, publishing, or high finance. You'll create new business systems that generate great profit for many people. You'll blossom as a CEO or entrepreneur and eventually launch a foundation that funds causes you believe in.

VIRGO 9 PATH: You'll eventually step up to your role as physician, global ambassador, linguist, or founder of an alternative energy firm that helps third-world countries. Don't get stuck in past disappointments or only see the flaws of humanity. You need to focus on the future and move forward in solving global problems. You would also be a gifted spiritual coach or grief counselor.

VIRGO 11 PATH: You're here to enlighten us with insight and grace. Find your niche by teaching higher math, science, or the arts. Your books, films, and photographs will shed light on the global problems we need to solve.

VIRGO 22 PATH: It may take awhile to live up to your mission of teaching the world new and better ways to solve everyday problems— from teaching people to find meaningful work to teaching organic farming or working in healthcare. But you will get there eventually, and your inspired ideas will change the way we live.

LIBRA (SCALES) = SEPTEMBER 23–OCTOBER 23

Grace, beauty, truth, and fairness flavor your mission. Rather than focus on injustices, you'll create solutions. Your abundant talents will find a home in the arts, whether you choose acting, dance, writing, or design.

LIBRA 1 PATH: Standing up for what you believe in is your mission. But you'll do it with a gracious, artistic flair through dance, writing, or acting. You'll thrive as a consultant in the fashion and beauty industries, as an independent-minded writer who has an elegant perspective on life, or as the founder of an awe-inspiring dance troupe.

LIBRA 2 PATH: Your voice and presence will naturally comfort others. Instead of burying yourself in the details of life, use your intuition and hypersensitivity to help those in pain. Don't let childhood emotional scars damage your ability to heal loved ones. Whether you teach gardening or become an intuitive therapist, your sensitivities are your healing gifts.

LIBRA 3 PATH: If you're not a dancer, you'll be a writer or painter. Creating beauty with your never-ending talents and sharing your viewpoint with the world (in a way that uplifts and inspires) is your lifelong mission. To make money you can write or be a fashion stylist or designer. Ultimately you'll express those lofty, brilliant ideas as a teacher, political advocate for the arts, or fiction writer and lead the world to a new paradigm—if you're up for the full potential of your path.

LIBRA 4 PATH: Is there anything more beautiful than the grace of Libra wrapped around the steely strength of the 4? I don't think so. Your impossible combination of beauty, grace, and determination makes you unstoppable in everything you do—from law to book publishing or dance. Remember not to get lost in the hard work.

LIBRA 5 PATH: With more beauty, talent, and charisma than you know what to do with, you'll be tempted to push the limits of sensory indulgence until you find your center. Someday you'll realize that your beauty and talent are on purpose; and its purpose is to raise the vibration of the planet. Teaching languages, writing about the arts, acting, or selling products that promote healthy lifestyle are all good fits.

LIBRA 6 PATH: Your passion for fairness and justice will probably send you into law or politics. But unless you're directly helping people, you'll be unhappy. As a physician or chiropractor you can use your healing touch to soothe those in pain. Ultimately your work as an alternative healer, therapist, or art teacher will fulfill you most.

LIBRA 7 PATH: If ever there was a path of beauty and grace, this is it. Your energy and charm will knock people over. Use that charisma to promote the arts or to help others find their artistic power. Your brilliant mind demands that your work be meaningful; eventually you'll move from acting or design into your role as teacher, writer, or mentor.

LIBRA 8 PATH: You are a born entrepreneur, so the sooner you own your power in the world of money and business, the better. Start your beauty product business, film production company, or book-publishing venture while you're young. Don't be swayed by loved ones telling you to work for other people. Yours is the path of big money and success, but only when you run the show. Go for it!

LIBRA 9 PATH: Your success will be first in theater and later as a writer, philanthropist, and medical humanitarian. Your vision of global justice will pull you to a career that we'll be reading about in the New York Times. The only pitfall will be if you rest on your charisma, indulge yourself, and spend too much time licking your wounds. But once you're over that, helping those in need will keep you moving forward.

LIBRA 11 PATH: Everyone will love you from the get-go, which is both good and bad. You're here to share the arts and heal people intuitively. Use your gifts to teach the more important lessons, such as spirituality, rather than the mundane, like software. Tell stories that inspire, direct movies that enlighten, and create artwork that opens our eyes.

LIBRA 22 PATH: You may decide to focus on the injustices you see around you—as a lawyer, journalist, or politician. But art, fiction, and the stage will always beckon. The world will benefit from your artistic gifts. Use them to shine light on the struggles of human life and inspire people to make great changes.

SCORPIO (SCORPION) = OCTOBER 24–NOVEMBER 21

No matter what you're here to accomplish, this sun sign will flavor your path with intensity, sexuality, and charisma. Use those gifts to shed light on the unseen world and guide others through traumatic pain—which doesn't intimidate you. Your insightful visions carry a depth of understanding that the world needs to embrace. Step up to it, tell your story, and don't wallow in disappointments.

SCORPIO 1 PATH: Leading others to sensual, physical healing is your work, whether you become a hands-on healer or a sex therapist. Don't be ashamed of who you are; wear it proudly, and create new ways for people to live sensually and healthily in this repressed world.

SCORPIO 2 PATH: Your gift is healing relationships—whether you choose a career as a couples counselor, sex therapist, intuitive healer, or high school health teacher. You'll empower others with your helpful insights and compassionate wisdom. Don't let that amazing intuition turn in on itself and cause you to be too sensitive, or you'll waste time getting your feelings hurt.

SCORPIO 3 PATH: Play until you're worn out. Then it's time to teach and write. Your brilliant mind and intense charisma will make you successful at any career, from politics to journalism to education. Creating beauty, whether it's as a fashion stylist or an interior designer, will be easy work. But your greatest work will be writing, teaching, and communicating new ideas that change the way we live.

SCORPIO 4 PATH: Your combination of strength, determination, and great charisma could lead to successful careers in dance, sports, or acting. But your love of hard work and fascination with the human body may pull you to medical school, where you'll blossom helping others.

SCORPIO 5 PATH: Your openness, passion for life, intense charisma, and love of adventure may push you to the limits of self-indulgence. When you eventually find your center through spirituality or family, you'll settle down. But don't ever try to fit into a box. Your true work is guiding others to explore the boundaries of their own worlds, whether that means as a doctor of divinity, mountain guide, shaman, filmmaker, or teacher of the culinary arts. Embrace your passion for adventure and share it with others.

SCORPIO 6 PATH: You may launch your career as a sensuous dancer, choreographer, or musician. Eventually you'll use your talents to heal the human body, instead of molding and shaping it for the stage. As a trauma therapist you'll move with clients to help them express and heal their pain, and music will be part of your great healing work. As a veterinarian you will work miracles with your healing touch.

SCORPIO 7 PATH: Pristine, intuitive, and refined, you'll be unhappy in a bustling corporate environment. You'll need lots of solace to find your way. But once you're working from your ivory tower, and only occasionally mingling with the masses, you'll feel better. Writing books from home, designing inspiring architecture, teaching medicine, or being a psychotherapist would suit you.

SCORPIO 8 PATH: Early on you'll recognize your ability to use sensuality to have power over others. Growing up, you may even experience sexual abuse—as you observe the right and wrong uses of sexual power. Eventually you'll use that knowledge to educate and lead others—as an emergency room physician, rape crisis center director, or the founder of an enterprise that creates products for health and beauty.

SCORPIO 9 PATH: It doesn't get much better than this combination. You have all the charisma you need to open any door, from music to theater or politics—as long as you don't wallow in your pain. In your early life you may be tempted to get lost in the world of self-indulgence. But you will emerge and ultimately prosper in your role as humanitarian and healer. Start by becoming a teacher, forensics expert, or physician, and the rest will unfold.

SCORPIO 11 PATH: Your vibrational frequency is so high that most people think you're a "bit much." But that energy is on purpose; whether you're channeling in the most passionate musical talent or helping people live up to their greatest potential as an intuitive therapist, your high frequency is needed on this planet. Don't try to fit in; instead be happy to stand out, in a place where your intuitive, healing gifts will be recognized. Good careers include music, education, becoming a veterinarian, or alternative medicine.

SCORPIO 22 PATH: With your power and personal charisma opening doors for you, from finance to medicine and law, it may be difficult to find your true path. Once you quit trying to fit in, and allow yourself to become the visionary healer you are, the world will be your eager audience. Your great work will transform health, finance, and politics.

SAGITTARIUS (ARCHER) = NOVEMBER 22–DECEMBER 21

You're the only soul who truly relishes a party and can start up a conversation with anyone—from the president of the United States to a computer nerd. Yet don't let your social personality pull you from your mission and sidetrack you into wasting too much time on superficiality. Your social gifts are on purpose, to help you succeed as a teacher and visionary.

SAGITTARIUS 1 PATH: You're a gifted speaker and teacher, and if you choose a corporate setting, become the trainer who inspires from the stage or the manager who leads teams to success with your social charisma. Learn to go within, follow your heart, and function not only from your head. Eventually you'll start a networking or training business.

SAGITTARIUS 2 PATH: Make your living as a teacher or therapist—you'll be paid to indulge your passion for talking to people all day long. Never work alone in a cubicle or get lost in the details of computer work. Your mission is to connect with others, and those connections feed your soul. Create a networking group, become a life coach, or teach a class of chatty middle schoolers, and you'll be on path.

SAGITTARIUS 3 PATH: As the life of the party and smartest girl in the class, you'll need to settle down and focus on one subject to find your path, even though you love learning everything from science to art. Once you choose a subject, teach it. Your gift with words and writing will bring greater understanding to anything from interior design to biology. Though you may enjoy event planning and be quite successful at it, true fulfillment will come from teaching and making a difference.

SAGITTARIUS 4 PATH: Hardworking, down-to-earth, and great with people, you'll thrive in any career from engineering to architecture to journalism. Your people skills will get you in the door, and your hard work and fierce determination will make you successful. But don't lose yourself in the hard work. When you spend all day pushing papers or building homes, you're not using your gift for social networking. Pick up the phone, interview people, make a sales call, get out of the office and into the classroom or conference room, where your gifts will truly blossom.

SAGITTARIUS 5 PATH: You'll be the last to leave the party, but once you do, your good work can begin, such as teaching, writing, and coaching. You'll be drawn to sales and marketing, where you'll prosper. But your challenge is to find your center and quit trying to please everyone. Once you've mastered that, show others how. After the wild and wonderful life you've led, people will clamor to hear your inspiring story.

SAGITTARIUS 6 PATH: You'll probably start a cohousing community, dance company, acting troupe, or alternative school for children. Your work will always be insightful and compassionate. Choose teaching or become a family therapist so that you can put your healing gifts and great people skills to good use.

SAGITTARIUS 7 PATH: Your challenge is to balance your outgoing, highly social personality with your intellectually and intuitively focused higher work. You're bound to have some confusing times as you navigate this. Are you a party planner or a spiritual teacher? Are you a graphic designer or a therapist? Your soul-reinvention turning points will get you back on path, which is focused on the higher meaning of life and translating that for others as a writer, minister, or teacher. In the meantime write stories that reveal our intuitive connections, or design soul maps that enlighten us. Ultimately your work will be focused on the divine one way or another.

SAGITTARIUS 8 PATH: Your extraordinary people skills, coupled with your likable, wide-ranging personality, will make you successful at anything from business to sports. Careers in sports broadcasting, marketing, or television will allow your gifts to blossom. Finally you'll see the purpose in this potent combination as a coach or teacher helping others to find their power.

SAGITTARIUS 9 PATH: Your mission is service, and your gift is the ability to talk to anyone from any country in any language; you'll spearhead large humanitarian efforts and run global foundations. Travel as soon as you can, teach English as a second language, and think big, but don't stray from your core purpose of service. Abundance will come to you with little need for struggle, as long as you're on path. Don't bother trying to be conventional.

SAGITTARIUS 11 PATH: Your hypersensitivity and deep intuition can be buried beneath your charismatic, outgoing personality. People will like you and not realize how unusual your gifts are—until they get to know you. Your divine mastery of human understanding will help you find your niche as teacher, therapist, writer, and guide for the less enlightened.

SAGITTARIUS 22 PATH: Politics will call you from a young age, but you may choose speaking to corporate executives or performing Shakespeare instead. Whichever stage you pick, be sure to speak your own ideas, and share your unique visions of how to make life better for all of us. You are one of those folks who actually can change the world. The good news is that you'll have fun doing it.

CAPRICORN (GOAT) = DECEMBER 22–JANUARY 19

You came here to immerse yourself in the earthy, practical details of day-to-day reality. That gift of perseverance and sure-footed determination, coupled with your intense focus on what you want, will get you up any mountain—no matter how lofty your mission may be.

CAPRICORN 1 PATH: Stubborn and practical, you can build, edit, create from the ground up, and teach others to do the same. Your mission is earthy and strong; build houses, edit novels, navigate expeditions, or create dances. Always be true to your own vision.

CAPRICORN 2 PATH: Your intense attention to detail will pull you to newsroom editing or writing software. But your higher work will be teaching others to read, write, or design software. As a coach or counselor, you can help your clients organize the insurmountable details of their lives.

CAPRICORN 3 PATH: Whether you're a potter, chef, or dancer, you'll put physical form to your creative instincts. Ultimately, words and ideas will pull you. You'll write childrens' books and fantasy fiction and someday teach others how to write. Make it fun, or you won't stick with it for long. Teaching in alternative settings will be more comfortable than in traditional public schools, where your creativity is likely to be stifled.

CAPRICORN 4 PATH: Your tremendous strength and practicality will probably have you climbing mountains or running touchdowns from a very young age. Someday, you'll create systems for huge businesses to rest on—whether you become the COO, a systems engineer, or a hardworking administrative assistant. Eventually you'll realize your gift for editing and journalism, and you may spend much of your career in some form of publishing.

CAPRICORN 5 PATH: Focus on mastering the tangible pleasures of life—from food to music, theater, or dance. If you choose to go corporate, try sales and marketing, where you'll feel less confined. As a culinary expert, food or travel writer, musician, or massage therapist, you'll be successful and fulfilled.

CAPRICORN 6 PATH: Your desire to help others in a hands-on way will be evident at an early age. Make career choices that allow you to do that, such as physician, chiropractor, nutritionist, or acupuncturist, rather than do administrative work in a medical office. Go to graduate school and get that master's degree so you can heal others for a living and not get stuck in the mundane details of office work.

CAPRICORN 7 PATH: As a lab researcher, graphic designer, or financial analyst, your brilliance and ability to focus on details will make you highly successful. Find a higher sense of purpose by pursuing spiritual knowledge so the mundane details don't drain you. Later in life, you'll teach science and write enlightening books that help people navigate their lives from a higher perspective.

CAPRICORN 8 PATH: As an entrepreneur, your company will create practical products that organize and consolidate our busy lives. Don't hide behind your need to be realistic and conventional and not step up to your power. Once you're at the helm of the ship, your attention to details will attract success and wealth. Your happiness will come from sharing that knowledge and abundance with others through teaching, coaching, mentoring, or writing.

CAPRICORN 9 PATH: Whether you choose to teach culinary skills, design inspiring energy-efficient homes, become a grief counselor, or run a nonprofit foundation, you're here to help others. Don't get lost in the details of figuring out which spices are best for which dish. Instead focus on the big picture of feeding hungry children through your innovative culinary programs and training volunteers to supply food and housing to victims of natural disasters.

CAPRICORN 11 PATH: As an inspired software designer or graphic computer artist, you'll find success and abundance. Remember, though, it's not just about the things. Your path is about people, too. When you stop tinkering with gadgets, you'll recognize your gift for healing and inspiring others with new ideas. As a politician, teacher, or author, you'll find your ultimate work.

CAPRICORN 22 PATH: Embrace the bigger picture of life, move away from details and drudgery, and become the hands-on teacher you're meant to be—with a voice that makes a difference in the world. You may decide to be a green builder or publish a magazine that promotes holistic living. Either way, focus on new ideas that inspire the world to live more authentically.

AQUARIUS (WATER BEARER) = JANUARY 20–FEBRUARY 18

Your ability to teach and inspire others is paramount on this path. Use these great strengths to change the world. Cultivating new ideas is essential for you. Take classes, read great books, surround yourself with thought-provoking people. Education will help you move from the mundane to the philosophical.

AQUARIUS 1 PATH: This is a path for great leaders; through politics, the arts, or education you can inspire the entire world to a new way of thinking. Never compromise your vision; if you take the corporate path choose training or management tracks—or you'll sabotage anyone who tries to be your boss. It's better for you to be the rebel leader than the unhappy, belligerent drone.

AQUARIUS 2 PATH: Your lucky spouse will enjoy spending many hours discussing relationships, ideas, and the meaning of life. Don't be too didactic, though, or you'll become a bore. Bring those great ideas into your work as a philosophy or history teacher, relationship therapist, or inspired software designer.

AQUARIUS 3 PATH: Whether you choose teaching children to read or adults to speak another language, you'll thrive in a classroom. Take writing and language courses early on. Enjoy your creative and brilliant journey, but don't depend too much on others for financial support. Step up to the front of the room and teach us what comes naturally to you, and you'll be right on path.

AQUARIUS 4 PATH: Your hunger for finding better ways of working will help you become the general contractor, project manager, or mountaineering instructor. You'll quickly rise to the top as head engineer, where your intelligent systems will provide a solid foundation for new homes or businesses.

AQUARIUS 5 PATH: Life is a huge canvas waiting for you to paint it with your colorful adventures, from teaching scuba diving and mountaineering to becoming an alternative health practitioner. Live loud and large, and never get lost in convention. You'll shut down your higher self whenever you try to fit in. Life coaching is a natural fit, as is teaching languages, because they expand our greater understanding of the world.

AQUARIUS 6 PATH: You're a gifted healer, and you'll thrive as a family physician or therapist. You'll bring new ideas and artistic vision to groups, communities, and ultimately the world as you step into your teaching mission. Don't give away your power by catering to the needs of others. Find your center and move forward courageously. You'll do amazing work—once you own up to who you are.

AQUARIUS 7 PATH: Your hunger for new ideas and higher knowledge, along with your need to teach and inspire, will push you to academics, quantum physics, metaphysics, and philosophy. You'll thrive in a career that lets you write and teach the higher knowledge you've mastered. Graduate school will help you blossom. If you venture into the corporate world, do so only as a teacher-trainer. Graphic design and Jungian psychotherapy will interest you. In later years you'll add writing to your skill repertoire.

AQUARIUS 8 PATH: Whether you work in politics to change health care or create a TV show that inspires people to improve their lives, you'll need to find a large outlet for your mission. As an entrepreneur you'll inspire others to succeed. Your media companies will thrive with their innovative educational products, and your enlightened approach to business will leave a legacy of abundance.

AQUARIUS 9 PATH: If anyone came to save the world, it's you. To serve and teach where you're needed most should be your mantra. Don't worry about financial gain; everything you need will come to you. You may start in the arts and move into politics or humanitarian work. Directing a nonprofit foundation or a career in journalism are great fits for you.

AQUARIUS 11 PATH: You'll be drawn to acting, or you may choose to channel your gifts into politics, teaching, and writing. If you stay in theater, your ability to uplift audiences will make you famous and wealthy. Following the path of medicine would allow you to pioneer new healing modalities that change the way we treat disease.

AQUARIUS 22 PATH: Your brilliance, charisma, and power will help you thrive in the business world, but when you're ready, your real mission reveals itself. As a visionary teacher or politician, you'll create new systems that alleviate suffering or put an end to illiteracy.

If you stay in business, your inspired ideas could transform management.

PISCES (FISH) = FEBRUARY 19–MARCH 20

Profound intuition and innate spiritual wisdom are your gifts, no matter what your mission is. Whenever you stifle that intuition in order to fit in, you're off path. Be sure to focus those intense feelings on the highest wisdom, and stay well above darkness and ignorance.

PISCES 1 PATH: You're here to lead brilliantly, and you'll rise like cream to the top, wherever you go. As a CEO, world-class mountain guide, or publisher, your leadership style is inspired intuition. You'll eventually teach others to find their own intuitive guidance. This shift happens when you learn to use your sensitivity as a gift rather than a burden.

PISCES 2 PATH: Your challenge will be finding your center so the everyday onslaught of feelings, intuitions, and sensitivities you pick up don't overwhelm you. How will you use that intense awareness to help others rather than be wounded by your hypersensitivity? Only by learning to connect with your higher self every day. Then you will shine in your role as a great intuitive, healer, or teacher.

PISCES 3 PATH: As an artist or dancer, you'll delight audiences with your unique and playful visions. Being intuition based, you may shy away from higher education. Eventually you'll own your power as a designer or language teacher. Ultimately you'll teach intuitive arts— whether you call that healing or spirituality.

PISCES 4 PATH: I would hire you to run my business in a heartbeat, since you're able to combine hard work and fierce determination with intuition. That rare combination of talents makes you an intuitive architect, journalist, or office manager. Either way it's powerful stuff. So don't be afraid to rely on gut feelings in whichever career you choose.

PISCES 5 PATH: You lack the filters and boundaries that most people have—which is a gift and a challenge. That openness can be overwhelming, but don't shut down. You're on path whenever you're living fearlessly instead of holding back. Your mission requires traveling, exotic adventures, sensuality, passion, and someday teaching others to navigate their emotional terrain. As an actor or healer you'll thrive. Careers in film directing, music, or alternative medicine are all good choices.

PISCES 6 PATH: Your antennas are huge and pick up everything—even things you don't want to see. But when you're ready, you'll step up to the great work of being a powerful healer and using your clairvoyance to help others. Until then you'll find comfort in the arts as a dancer or painter. To start out in the right direction, get your degree in education or psychology.

PISCES 7 PATH: As a writer, photographer, or designer you'll do well. Eventually you'll own up to your ability to sense everything and guide others to that higher knowledge. Without any filters to protect you, life can be overwhelming. But your brilliant mind will guide you, whether you own up to being a psychic or hide it behind the acceptable label of therapist.

PISCES 8 PATH: You're a gentle, intuitive leader and entrepreneur. You'll start businesses and attract great financial success once you step into your power. Start your own media company, publish books or greeting cards, or run a psychic arts school. Just don't let your sensitivities stop you from being the boss.

PISCES 9 PATH: Beauty, grace, charisma, intuition, wisdom—you've got it all. Just don't rest on your charisma. Now's the time to use your power and wisdom on the stage or in the arts; ultimately you'll serve the world as a global humanitarian and healer.

PISCES 11 PATH: Your acute sensitivity may cause you great pain while growing up. You truly DO know what others are thinking—for better or worse. But there's a career in that. This is the path of the divine intuitive—whether you channel it into the arts or medicine. You're here to serve the world with your heightened awareness of what's needed.

PISCES 22 PATH: You're an old soul here to change the world with your wise insights. You could choose acting, novel writing, or screenwriting to tell your stories. Channel that powerful intuition into very practical subjects like career, health, and money—and your work will help humanity evolve to its highest good.

TO SUMMARIZE THIS CHAPTER

◆ Your astrological sun sign reveals the flavor of your work mission. Someone who is on a 7 path with an Aries sun sign will fulfill their destiny with a different style than someone on a 7 path with a Pisces sun sign.

◆ By understanding your birth path and the sun sign flavor that you wrapped around it, you will get more specific ideas about your true work.

Try it now:

Your birth-path number:

Your sun sign:

Insights and ideas:

10

YOUR CURRENT
CAREER CYCLE

Bᴇᴛʜ ᴡᴀꜱ ᴀ ᴛʜɪʀᴛʏ-ꜱᴇᴠᴇɴ-ʏᴇᴀʀ-ᴏʟᴅ (Gemini 8 path) management consultant. When she first contacted me she was in the midst of her 9 personal year. The management career she had relied on for nine years was ending. Her entire department of coworkers was being laid off, her marriage was in trouble, and she had no clarity about her next step.

Beth's Gemini 8 path mission meant that her potent combination of leadership and brilliance was well suited for management consulting. Her work had been on path. But when we explored the meaning of the 9 personal year she was experiencing, everything made more sense. Letting go and reinvention were required. It was time to step up to the next level of her work.

"So I'm not doing something wrong," she said with relief. "This isn't about me not making the right choices."

"No. What's required of you now is releasing the old, tapping into your highest wisdom—however you define that—and knowing that the next step becomes clear when you move into the beginning of your next nine-year cycle, which starts in January."

"That's probably why I enrolled in a class to become a financial adviser, but just couldn't get myself to go."

"Yes, it's not time for beginning new things yet. You need to clean out your closet first—throw out your old clothes (ideas, patterns, careers, and relationships) so you have room for the new. Think of the way this works in nature: First you have to turn over the soil and make it ready for planting in the spring. Then you have to wait to be sure the temperature won't freeze again. If you plant too early your crops won't grow."

Our discussions helped Beth spend the next few months exploring her options, processing new ideas, deepening her spiritual center, and researching new directions we discovered. It comforted her to know that she didn't need to pressure herself to have the perfect answer right away.

In January, just as her 1 personal year started, she was offered a position as CEO of a newly formed think tank that focuses on the exact issues she's passionate about—teaching leaders and executives to use their power wisely. This offer came after she had done months of soul-searching that made it clear she needed to be a CEO, loved facilitating leadership, and was ready for a new venture. She had networked with these goals in mind—which led her to the group planning the think tank. When their offer came she was ready to move forward, and she took the job. She's now working happily in this next phase of her meaningful work.

Also during her 9 personal year, she and her husband spent a few days away from home at a spiritual retreat center, where they started a new dialogue about their future. They processed several unspoken and unresolved issues that needed to be dealt with. It cleared the slate so they could begin anew.

Since then, she reports, their marriage is much stronger.

As her story illustrates, Beth experienced the cleansing benefits of a 9 personal year; it changed a work situation that needed to change so she could step up to the next level, and it helped reinvent her marriage. Our nine-year cycles are intended to keep us from getting too far off path. When we're forced to reexamine and reinvent every nine years, it assures steady growth and transformation. At each turning point we become more authentically focused on the work we came to do.

However, this turning point is not always easy.

Many clients first contact me when they're in the midst of a 9 personal year, and they're not happy campers. Circumstances they've relied on for years are falling apart. Relationships are changing, and it's getting painfully obvious that big change is required.

More often than not people get scared and angry at this point and look around for someone to blame. Its takes tremendous courage and inner work to accept the idea that your higher self set this crisis up— so that you would change directions.

Instead you may listen to friends and family who say: "Yeah, you're having some bad luck. Life is tough. Hang in there, and keep trying to make it work." They'll probably encourage you to keep going in the same direction until your luck changes for the better.

So you decide to dig in and refuse to reinvent. You hang on to the job that doesn't fit, or if you walk away from it you get another one just like it. And the more you fight the change, the worse things get.

Does this sound familiar?

What if you tried to do things a little differently? What if you understood that these reinvention moments are the greatest opportunities you could ask for in a lifetime? They're your chance to get back on path, accomplish your mission, and live up to your full potential.

You don't have to believe me about this. Pythagoras, founder of our modern number system, described these cycles of change back in 580 B.C.

WHERE ARE YOU IN
THE NINE-YEAR CYCLE OF CHANGE?

No matter what birth path you're on, for every year of your life you've been under the vibrational influence of a particular number—1 through 9 or 11 or 22. Since all of our learning takes place within the vibrational range of these numbers, you're working with a different type of energy each year, within a repeating nine-year cycle. After each nine-year cycle is complete, a new one begins, bringing the benefits and burdens of the last cycle into the new one.

This is all on purpose, of course. It's part of your plan. As you look back on your life, tracing these nine-year cycles, you'll see the repeating patterns of change in your life. You'll realize how you've gotten better at mastering certain challenges over time. And you've gotten better at letting go of the things you need to release in a 9 personal year.

You started this lifetime in the vibration of the path you've chosen. If your birth path is the number 5, then the first year of your life was a 5 personal year. The second year of your life was a 6 personal year, and so on. By adding up your day, month, and year of birth, you'll find your destined birth-path number as well as the personal year that began your journey. You've repeated these nine-year cycles throughout your life.

In this chapter, we're going to determine where you are in that nine-year cycle and what that means to your career.

Your current personal year is determined by the single-digit numbers of your birth month and birth date added to the current calendar year and reduced to a single digit (or a master number 11 or 22).

For example, someone with a birthday of September 15, 1951—during the year 2009—would be experiencing an 8 personal year.

Birth month: September equals 9
Birth date: 15 = 6 (1 + 5 = 6)
Current year: 2009 equals 2 (2 + 0 + 0 + 9 = 11 = 1 + 1 = 2)

Add 9 (birth month) + 6 (birth date) + 2 (current year) to get personal
   year:
9 + 6 + 2 = 17 = 1 + 7 = 8
Personal year = 8

Even though this person would be experiencing an 8 personal year
during the calendar year 2009, by September 2009, they would feel
the beginnings of their 9 personal year (which coincides with the calendar year 2010).

Let's compute your personal year here:

Your birth month:
Your birth date:
Current year:

Total:

Reduced to a single digit:

This is your personal year:

What does this mean for your career? Here's a broad overview of the
vibrations of each personal year:

PERSONAL YEAR 1

This is an important new beginning: Launch your business, get a new job or title, start a graduate program, or move to a new location. Everything you do this year will influence the events of your life for the next nine years. There's lots of new energy helping you change directions. There's never been a better time for reinvention. This is also a year of intense self-focus, personal development, and cultivation of talents. Everything evolves around you and is dependent upon you. Have the courage to make important decisions and move forward bravely—like a pioneer. At times you may feel alone, but this year demands that you work mostly alone. Avoid starting trivial relationships now, because they will linger with you for the rest of your nine-year cycle.

PERSONAL YEAR 2

This is the year for cooperating with others to develop the vision you started last year. It's a slower, more gestative year, nurturing what you've already started rather than launching new things. Collect and assimilate data, and organize details. Your success hinges on working with and cooperating with others. Be receptive. Soften the forceful energy you thrived on last year. You might feel highly sensitive this year and develop warm friendships—even romances.

PERSONAL YEAR 11

In this highly charged year of personal illumination, your intellect is capable of achieving its greatest capacity—as well as intense psychic perception and artistic creation. Inspiration and revelation are yours to create with. The spiritual, psychic, and artistic are your focus, and meditation or prayer will enhance all of your gifts. Refine your tastes, collect art, associate with creative people. This is not your best year for commercial success, but rather for the inner evolution of your spiritual, intuitive, and artistic gifts.

PERSONAL YEAR 3

This is a social, playful year, full of social events and new interests. Express yourself, get into the center of things, entertain groups. Forget long-term planning and just enjoy life; don't make important decisions about your future. The performing arts will call you, and it's time to look your best. Develop your skills with words, written or spoken. Life is your stage—enjoy it! Whatever you started in your 1 year is now reaping enjoyment for you. It's your year to blossom.

PERSONAL YEAR 4

It's time to get to work in this serious and responsible year. Get practical, establish organization and efficiency systems, build the foundation for future growth, set a budget, and do the physical work. Focus on the physical details of getting your home in order—whether that means moving, remodeling, or cleaning. Engage in fitness and sports activities. Dependability and responsibility are your keys to success.

PERSONAL YEAR 22

This year your greatest aspirations and inspirations will be put into practical reality. You'll be bringing your most advanced ideas to a realistic and workable form. Humanity and society as a whole will benefit from your work, if you choose to step up to the plate. It's a year of putting personal concerns aside and doing your best for the world at large. Make big plans and introduce enormous changes. By focusing on the positive vibrations of this number, you'll have the opportunity to ascend to your greatest career achievements and acquire abundant financial rewards. You'll also feel the sting of criticism that greatness attracts. Focus on your work and keep moving forward.

PERSONAL YEAR 5

Get ready for expansion, adventure, and the unexpected in this turning-point year. During this fast-moving, action-packed time, you'll be happiest and doing your best work when everything is changing around you. Take trips, investigate opportunities, and get rid of anything that is monotonous or boring. Eliminate conditions and people that are holding you back. Make room for the new. Focus on freedom and adapting to change. Enjoy this sensual year with many opportunities for physical indulgence. You'll be supercharged, attractive, and sexual. Revive your relationships or work circumstances with new energy.

PERSONAL YEAR 6

In this more responsible year you'll take care of the important people in your life and career. Rather than focus on yourself, you'll adjust to the needs of others and enjoy group activities as you shift away from the sensual and passionate excesses of the 5 year. Marriage and close friendships will blossom due to your efforts to understand the people in your life. Let go of superficiality and take responsibility for yourself and others. Yet don't take on more than you can carry, or you'll fall into depression and be overwhelmed. This is one year, though, when general harmony is more important than your own needs.

PERSONAL YEAR 7

Enjoy this sabbatical from the physical aspects of life, and focus your attention on the study of abstract ideas, science, mysticism, spirituality, and artistic endeavors. Withdraw from the center of things and write books, go to school, meditate, and do research. Refine what you began in this nine-year cycle by analyzing and perfecting projects, relationships, and goals. In this quiet introspective year, you'll do best spending lots of time alone and allowing change to occur naturally rather than forcing it. Your intuition will be at its most powerful—rely on it for all decisions. Pursue nothing; you will naturally attract what is meant to be in your life.

PERSONAL YEAR 8

The serenity and reflection of the 7 year is over as you jump headfirst into the world of career, power, and money. If you wrote a book last year, this is the year to promote and sell it. If you researched and developed your new business last year, now is the time to get it funded. Physical accomplishment and material success are your focus as you reap the seeds of success that you planted early in this nine-year cycle. During this powerful year claim recognition and take command to get concrete results. Think big, manage and direct others, move forward. Yet beware of abusing your power or becoming greedy. Be patient and generous to others, even if that feels tedious.

PERSONAL YEAR 9

This year you will wrap up what you started in your 1 year. Lingering relationships will surface to be examined, then kept or discarded for the next cycle. Your career will conclude the focus that it's had for the past nine years, even though you won't see the new cycle just yet. Open your hands and let go, with faith that something new and better will arrive in your 1 year. You may be fired or laid off or simply come to the end of a project you've worked on for years. Relationships will fall away or be transformed; and you'll grieve for your losses over the past nine years. Peace comes from higher wisdom and a greater connection to spirituality. The larger lessons of life will call to you, and your insights will be heightened. Use this awareness to benefit the people around you. Focus on artistic and spiritual disciplines, and wait for the new inspiration that begins soon in your approaching 1 year.

YOUR TWO MOST POWERFUL (AND PAINFUL) LIFE REINVENTIONS: AGES TWENTY-NINE AND FIFTY-EIGHT

Let's say you've done all the right things with your career; maybe you went to law school, got a job with a good firm, and now collect a nice paycheck and benefits. Yet the age of thirty is fast approaching and you feel like you're wearing the wrong skin. Your life doesn't fit who you are inside. But everyone around you is very proud of your accomplishments. You can't discuss your unhappiness with friends. They say, "Be grateful you have a job. The economy is terrible, and you won't find anything better than what you have."

Or maybe you've been successful at your career for many years, and the age of fifty-eight is fast approaching. You've built a respectable reputation at your trade, honed your skills, and are quite good at what you do. In fact you're rather attached to your prestigious title. Yet inside you're tormented. You toss and turn at night. The politics in your office are driving you mad, and you're having health problems.

Congratulations! You're right on schedule. If you're questioning everything about your life from career to relationships, this is on purpose. You preprogrammed these two major career reinventions into your lifetime, and you've just bumped into one.

Now you're going to wake up and remember who you are and what you came to do. These two turning points are what the astrologers call Saturn returnings. When they coincide with your personal 9 year, life flips upside down.

The first wake-up call hits most people between the ages of twenty-seven and thirty. You also have the end of your personal nine-year cycle falling in the midst of this upheaval. When you align your twenty-ninth birth year with your nearest 9 personal year, you'll see the pinnacle of this reinvention point. The unease you experience during this time is inevitable; you signed up for this challenge!

This exquisite pain is designed to force you to shed ideas, beliefs, and relationships that you've carried from childhood, in order to see more clearly the true mission and intent for your lifetime. You can no longer believe what was handed to you or be who you were expected to be.

And the more you cling to old beliefs and patterns, the more painful the transition gets.

The second Saturn returning occurs around the age of fifty-eight. When you line that age up with your nearest 9 personal year, you'll see your personal pinnacle of reinvention. This second Saturn returning is designed to strip you of worldly pretense accumulated through false definitions of self in the work world. If you've been identifying yourself as a brilliant software engineer, yet you're here to share your creative visions through books or film, your software career will come to an abrupt end. You'll be forced to look outside the box for your next career move.

Quit complaining about how confused you feel, and be grateful that your wise old higher self knew you would need these two major wake-up calls and preprogrammed them into your lifetime. The pain you feel is on purpose; it's your fuel for moving forward. If you don't use that pain to fuel your reinvention, you'll self-destruct (through depression, illness, drugs, alcohol, divorce, and the like).

The end result of this inner turmoil (when used for reinvention) is a happier career that's more aligned with your authentic self and what you came to accomplish. No one else did this to you, even if you've been fired, laid off, or broken up with. It's what your higher self intended. It's not the end of your world, it's just the beginning.

Now is the time to ask yourself the big questions: Why am I here? What gifts and talents did I bring with me to accomplish the mission? These questions will guide you to the first step of career change—whether that means investigating where you could teach law (if teaching is part of your mission), researching a different type of law practice (if that would be more in alignment with your authentic self), getting reeducated, or starting your own business.

Your new direction always builds on the things you've already done; your past experience and knowledge gets repackaged for the next career. Every course you've studied and every skill you've learned has been on purpose. Now it's time to reuse, recycle, and reinvent everything you know.

Please understand that you *did* come here with a mission—to raise the vibration of the planet in your unique way using your innate gifts and talents. This is also known as "work."

And that mission *does* require frequent reinventions. Stepping up to the next level of your great work is required several times during a lifetime—especially every nine years. But the biggest changes are the ones at ages twenty-nine and fifty-eight. This is when your higher self turns up the volume and yells: "Mission not yet accomplished!"

The turning point at fifty-eight can be the most challenging. My goodness, you've had an awesome career so far! You've raised kids. You're not just a nobody. Yet your life is in turmoil. You know inside that you haven't yet done your great work. You know you're here to make a difference—leave a larger legacy.

In your fifties it's time to peel off the false identity you've developed to succeed in the career world. Own your naked, authentic self in the world again, and do the sacred work you've already signed up for. Even if that means owning up to something you've never owned up to before.

Your higher self is telling you that you only have a few productive decades left, and it's now or never. When health issues happen in our fifties, it's just the soul nudging us to remember who we are.

It's your choice: Either choose to rise above your challenges and live up to the great potential you came here to accomplish, or sink beneath your pain and fear.

Either way it's your mission. There's no one to answer to for your success or failure but yourself. And, as you can tell from the way you feel at these transition points, your higher self is quite demanding. Be grateful for your preprogrammed mission, and move forward.

If you're currently in the middle of either of these career-life transitions, here are some steps to help you.

1. Meditate or pray at least twice a day to quiet your crazy thinking and tap into your higher self, which is where you'll find the answers you can trust. Meditation is the best way to tap into your inner GPS system.

2. Be grateful for this opportunity to reinvent, and be honest about how unhappy and off path you've been.

3. Raise your energy through little things like laughing, walking, and reading inspirational books. Raising your energy will help move you forward in a positive direction.

4. Dream of your amazing new life and career. What will it look like? Focus only on the future and what you want to happen next.

5. See a career intuitive/coach/counselor or take a career workshop to help you manage this transition.

6. Remember, a death is required before every rebirth. Let go. Surrender what you know. The new direction reveals itself only when you've let go of your old story.

TO SUMMARIZE THIS CHAPTER

◆ Your current personal year is determined by the single-digit numbers of your birth month and birth date added to the current calendar year and reduced to a single digit (or a master number 11 or 22).

Let's compute your personal year here:

Your birth month:
Your birth date:
Current year:

Total:

....

Reduced to a single digit:

This is your personal year:

◆ Your two most important life reinventions are around the ages of twenty-nine and fifty-eight. When you calculate your nine-year cycles and see where your 9 years overlap with the ages of twenty-nine and fifty-eight, you can see where these reinvention points peak.

11

THE TALENTS YOU
BROUGHT WITH YOU

Whenever everything is stripped away, who's left inside you? In those moments of deep, soul-searching surrender, walking alone on a beach contemplating your life, who do you remember being when you were happy? Were you authentic and sweet? Did you love playing music or writing stories that made people happy?

When all else falls away, are you someone who speaks the truth and perceives the essential? Or someone who takes charge and launches into business no matter the challenge? Whatever your answer, this core part of you reveals your innate talents—your most reliable clues to what you came to do.

Your talents are your only true compass in this lifetime; they'll diligently guide you to your mission. You brought them with you from the highest realms in order to use them to make the world a better place. And you've known what these gifts were since you were very young, but you may have been talked out of believing in them.

When your work fully uses these talents and is in alignment with your birth-path mission, you're absolutely on path. Then your work is successful and provides abundantly for you—against all odds—because you're on path. Your aligned vibration attracts success and abundance, no matter how unconventional your work is or how terrible the economy is. This is the law of divine order.

Getting your life lined up with your birth path and talents isn't as hard as you may think. Your intuition is constantly trying to push you in this direction; it's probably why you picked up this book.

In chapter 7 you identified your birth path—the mission you came to accomplish—along with the flavor of that mission as reflected in your sun sign. In chapter 10 we explored your nine-year cycles and discovered which number is influencing your career choices this year. Now we're going to examine the gifts you've carried with you since the early years of this lifetime. These are the things you love doing every day. They're the unique natural gifts that flow easily and gracefully through you.

They're different from your learned skills. You may have learned to write computer software, cook in a restaurant, or do bookkeeping. Those are skills you've learned in order to survive. But your talents are deeper. They're your graceful gift to the world, what comes most easily to you, and they're what you came here to share.

You may have downplayed your talents by saying that you're not "good enough" at them to succeed at making a living from them. Yes, developing those talents takes effort. But wouldn't you rather put effort into fully developing your gifts, so you can make your living doing something you love? Or would you prefer to put your hard work toward doing something you don't care about—just to get a paycheck? Which life would be more rewarding and successful for you? It's your choice.

Or perhaps you think your talents aren't unique. "Anybody can do what I can do," you might say. "If this gift is so graceful and effortless inside me, then why would it be hard for other people to do it?"

No one on this planet is on the exact same journey as you. No one has your exact blend of talents. The more often you share life stories with other people, the faster you'll realize this. Notice how different your childhood memories, dreams, successes, and failures are from those of your friends. Think about what you've always been great at yet didn't realize how unusual it was until now.

It's time to take a stand for your original mission and gifts. Get back to claiming your uniqueness so you can use those gifts to make the world a better place in your own way.

Tonight, before you go to sleep, spend a few minutes reviewing your life story from a detached perspective—as if you were watching a movie. Take note of the moments when you can say, "Look how good I was at that. . . ." Let those realizations guide you to the work you came here to do.

Once you clearly understand the unique vibration of your chosen path and how your talents interconnect with that path, you'll be empowered to accomplish your mission. For example, perhaps you're on the number 8 birth path and you've always loved thinking about ways to make money or dreaming up business ideas. But you didn't pursue those ideas because you thought it wasn't meaningful-enough work.

Recognize that you chose this path to learn something you needed to learn. Embrace your path passionately and accumulate wealth and power, so you can do great things for the world—such as funding non-profit foundations or creating camps for children with cancer. (That was the work of Paul Newman—a highly evolved 8-path soul.)

If your path is the number 7 and you've sometimes thought, I don't belong in this world of enterprise and frenetic activity, you've been right all along. You're here to study and analyze the higher knowledge of science, philosophy, psychology, art, or spirituality. Embrace that solitary, intuitive path and make your living from teaching or writing what you know. It's what you came here to do.

For most people the hardest part of finding your path is shutting out the voices that tell you what you should do and how you should fit in. When you see other people doing amazing things in the world, you may want to be like them. Being like anyone else except yourself will never lead to success or to the work you came to do.

When you study your early life, your childhood urges before you fell under the influence of societal pressures, you'll find the original intention of your unique path. Uncover it. Dust it off. And get back to your naked self.

If you're still having trouble identifying your innate talents, look to your birth path as a guide to what you may be naturally gifted at. For example:

BIRTH PATH 1 TALENTS:
Leadership, courage, clarity, and ability to invent new things and lead others to new ideas.

BIRTH PATH 2 TALENTS:
Ability to communicate well with others, be sensitive, put others at ease, and take care of details.

BIRTH PATH 3 TALENTS:
Ability to create or design beautiful things, express complex ideas brilliantly through words, visual arts, or dance.

BIRTH PATH 4 TALENTS:
Ability to build things, organize, work hard, focus, and overcome through determination.

BIRTH PATH 5 TALENTS:
Ability to embrace change, lead others to adventure and expansion, inspire with generosity of spirit, motivate, and share fearless sensual passion for life.

BIRTH PATH 6 TALENTS:
Ability to bring harmony and healing to groups and families, to bring beauty to the world through collaborative efforts.

BIRTH PATH 7 TALENTS:
Ability to analyze and understand complex concepts; to philosophize and contemplate science and the arts; to intuit, write, and teach spiritual principles.

BIRTH PATH 8 TALENTS:
Ability to attract and accumulate money and power through enterprise and use it for good in the world.

BIRTH PATH 9 TALENTS:
Ability to work for global issues, run nonprofits, write, speak, heal, and inspire others with humanitarian wisdom.

BIRTH PATH 11 TALENTS:
Ability to bring divine inspiration to share with humanity through the arts or through one-on-one counseling and instruction.

BIRTH PATH 22 TALENTS:
Ability to bring inspired, new, and highly evolved thinking to everyday challenges.

SALLY'S STORY

Sally was a screenwriter living in Los Angeles, married to a highly successful film producer. They had two kids, an enviable lifestyle, and a circle of powerful Hollywood friends. Yet her writing projects hadn't been successful in several years, and she was feeling lost. Her high-profile husband seemed successful at everything he did, while she felt adrift as the mother of two young children.

Sally was on the path of the refined number 7 with Sagittarius wrapped around it. Writing and directing were good choices for her career; she loved the solace of writing (a 7-path vibration), followed by the intense social contact of directing once the project found its funding (perfect for the Sagittarius energy). She especially loved making documentaries that made people think about life in a new way—which was very much on-path work for her.

After meditating on her mission I explained that the highest evolution of her path was to write films that showed the world a higher perspective on everyday life, using her gifts of wisdom and humor to enlighten us.

"It's so funny that you say my gifts are wisdom and humor. I asked my best friend yesterday what she thought my talents were and she said, 'Sharing your wisdom with humor.' That impressed me because that's the kind of writing I prefer anyway."

Because of Sally's 7 path, having time alone was essential for her happiness and creativity. She shouldn't feel guilty if she needed lots of time alone, I explained, even time away from the kids.

"I just can't be the popsicle mom who spends everyday doing art project with the kids," she whispered. "I see that all around me, and I just can't do it."

"On your path you need solitude and quiet time to tap into your intuition and spirituality in order to fuel your creative side. Without that solitude you'll feel drained emotionally and have nothing left to give," I explained.

"Hallelujah!" She laughed. "That's exactly how I feel."

We discussed writing projects that were currently on her plate and evaluated the merits of each one by asking if the finished project would show audiences a higher, more enlightened perspective on life through education, wisdom, and humor.

She was amazed to see how well that process of analysis explained *why some of her past projects had been successful and others hadn't. "We're here to work true to our mission, and when we do that we attract success—against all odds. When our work is off path, it won't be successful even if everyone says it will be," I told her.*

Months after our session I got an e-mail saying she had found a producer and funding for a comedy script she'd written. The main character was a woman who was having trouble finding her own power. She said that it fit her "mission" because it gave people a more enlightened way to look at life and love, using humor to illustrate the ideas. She was excited to tell me that the project was moving forward, and she was feeling happier and more centered.

"Now that I understand my path and talents, I can see the kind of projects I'm most successful at and why. This knowledge is invaluable to me."

MORE WAYS TO FIND YOUR TALENTS

1. Think about those things you love doing even on your days off—such as organizing a room, inspiring others to meet a goal, solving problems, or creating beautiful things. If you love doing crossword puzzles to solve challenging word problems, that's your natural analytical talent.

2. Remember the natural talents that you recognized in yourself as a child. Did you love writing in high school? Did you win school competitions for your science projects? All the things that come easily to us as children offer clues to our destined work.

3. Remember a time when you were very happy accomplishing something. You might have created a wonderfully successful wedding shower for your sister, and everyone raved about your creative ideas, decorations, and foods. It was

easy for you to do, and you felt inspired and happy doing it. Think about the parts of that accomplishment you most loved doing.

TO SUMMARIZE THIS CHAPTER

◆ Your talents are on purpose. You brought them with you to use in your great work, which raises the vibration of the planet in your unique way.

◆ Talents guide you to your great work. They are your most powerful compass for finding your mission.

◆ Talents are the things you love doing, come back to doing again and again in your lifetime, and they always come gracefully to you.

◆ Your top three talents are:

　　1.

　　2.

　　3.

◆ Are you currently using these talents every day in your job? If not, what can you do to change that?

12

IF IT MATTERS TO YOU, IT'S YOUR MISSION

R ANDY WAS ON A 1 birth path with Aquarius wrapped around
it. From a young age he had valued independence, autonomy,
and leadership—all core values that are intrinsically part of his lifetime mission on the 1 birth path. His first career choice was in alignment with this; he became a mountaineering and survival instructor
for Outward Bound School. He led people across the Colorado
Rockies—teaching them to overcome fears and limitations. He eventually traveled the world on mountaineering expeditions.

While visiting other countries Randy saw the poverty and suffering that existed in third-world countries from lack of education and
opportunities for self-improvement. When he hit a reinvention pe-
riod (a 9 personal year), he reevaluated what was most important to
him. He realized that leading people up mountains was no longer as
important as using his leadership to build schools and raise money
for the communities he had visited while traveling the world as a
climber.

His next career choices were in alignment with this desire to help others. He started a foundation to raise money that would create schools, and he eventually went into politics as a way of using his natural leadership abilities to make a global difference.

Randy's life illustrates how our values are part of our inner soul-navigation system.

When you chose your mission for this lifetime, your path carried with it a set of core values to help you stay on track and learn the lessons you intended to learn. For example, if you're on the path of the number 1, you value independence and autonomy—no matter what you do, where you work, or how much you change throughout the lifetime. That's because it's the basis of what you came to learn—how to be an independent being in the world and live true to your unique vision.

When you learned about your birth path in chapter 7, did it illuminate some core values that you've always had inside you?

However, other values *will* change during your lifetime to help you reinvent and get closer to your mission at each 9-year turning point.

Whatever feels deeply important to you today is on purpose: to guide you to the next step of your career journey—ultimately getting you to the work you came here to do.

When you examine your core values—the ones you carry with you throughout the lifetime—they show you the underlying mission of your lifetime.

When you understand your changing values due to life experiences, you'll see the next step to take on your career journey.

Here are some examples of how core values are reflected in the birth paths.

To be happy at work:

A 1 path values independence and being in charge.

A 2 path values working with others.

A 3 path values creativity, social interaction, and self-expression.

A 4 path values order, discipline, hard work, and practicality.

A 5 path values change, freedom, and adventure.

A 6 path values working with groups to promote harmony and beauty.

A 7 path values learning, analyzing, and higher knowledge.

An 8 path values money, success, and power—being in charge.

A 9 path values the highest humanitarian work in order to be happy.

An 11 path must have inspiration from people and the environment.

A 22 path must have work involving "new thinking" and inspired ideas.

These are core values. Your life and work should always be in harmony with these core values for you to be successful and happy. Yet your lifetime experiences will add a layer of different values to your list of what's important.

When evaluating your next career move, use the core values to keep you on path and the current values to guide your next step.

Is your life today in alignment with the core values that are most important to you?

When you meditate on this question, you may receive your most potent career guidance. Take a moment right now to contemplate what you value most in a career and how that lines up with the vibration of your birth path.

You can clarify your next career move by asking yourself, Will this new work satisfy my need to do such and such in the world?

If the answer is yes, take a step in that direction.

WHOM WOULD YOU MOST LIKE TO HELP?

Do you long to help people who feel unempowered or impoverished? Do you want to help those who suffer from physical illnesses such as cancer or diabetes? Does it move you to imagine helping children learn to speak or read effectively? Do you get fired up thinking about how you could help business people become more successful?

The truth is, your work is always serving someone. By getting in touch with those you long to help, the people your birth-path mission has set you up to help, your next career step is revealed.

Your birth-path number can help you find your perfect, most meaningful clients and customers.

For example, someone on a 1 birth path would be very effective teaching leadership to business executives. They're helping others find the leadership and independence that comes naturally to them. And they would be wonderful at helping people find their way from confusion and fear to clarity and confidence, since that has been their own journey.

A 2 birth path would be terrific at healing marriages, building teams, or teaching sensitivity to executives.

A 3 birth path can teach creativity, self-expression, and artistic skills to anyone who wants more beauty, joy, and authenticity in their life.

A 4 birth path can help people suffering from injustice, needing organizational help, or needing someone to get their project off the ground.

A 5 birth path can help anyone bring more adventure, travel, and sensuality into their lives. They would be especially helpful to burned-out executives needing an expanded view of life or to children needing courage.

A 6 birth path will bring harmony to any group, whether it's a community brought together through dance classes, a city inspired by a brilliantly designed building, a damaged family needing healing, or a downtrodden community needing education and hope.

A 7 birth path will be drawn to enlightening others through the arts, spirituality, science, or philosophy. They're gifted teachers to anyone seeking deeper understanding of scientific or spiritual principles.

An 8 birth path is divinely inspired at teaching business success, financial prosperity, and the ability to use power for good, such as in martial arts or medicine. They will be most helpful when offering their knowledge to less fortunate and powerless members of society.

A 9 birth path will be drawn to work for nonprofits that offer enlightened global principles. Planetary salvation will be their driving passion, and they can help anyone needing higher wisdom.

An 11 birth path will be drawn to heal and teach others one-on-one using their love of music and the arts. Their work will be aimed at helping individuals move past personal, emotional limitations.

A 22 birth path will long to do important work in the world that inspires the everyday person to live their day-to-day lives in a more enlightened and fearless manner.

YOUR INTENTION

Let's pull together some of the things you've contemplated so far. When we combine these ideas into an intention, we fire up our energy to attract opportunities that are in alignment with this vision. We are stating to the universe, "I'm ready to move forward. I'm ready to live up to my mission. I intend to use my unique talents of _____ in a way that's in harmony with my values of _____ and in alignment with my birth path, which is about _____."

JENNIFER'S STORY

When Jennifer, a thirty-five-year-old acupuncturist, walked into my office, I knew she was on the wrong path. Even though acupuncture is a profound healing method, she wasn't meant for it. She was on the path of the number 8 with Aquarius wrapped around it. That meant one thing: making great changes in large systems such as business, health care, and politics. She was already doing good work as a healer yet feeling depressed and frustrated because the venue was too small for her powerful energy.

"I know my healing work helps people, but it doesn't feel big enough, and I know that sounds silly. I'm constantly thinking about the larger problems of the world and how to solve them. I get bored seeing clients individually," she admitted during our session.

Her power was too overwhelming for a small private practice. People on the path of the number 8, like Jennifer, sometimes sabotage their work if it doesn't feel big or important enough.

By explaining her birth path, I helped her see what she had already signed up for—a strong mission to bring new ideas to the world. During my meditation on her birth date, I had seen her speaking in front of large groups about politics and health care. This vision was clearly from her long-term future, and I explained that now she only needed to focus on one little step at a time. She cried during most of the session—

nodding her head in agreement. We made a plan to change directions slowly.

Six months later I got this e-mail from her:

I just wanted to give you a little update on my life because I keep thinking of you while this transition is happening. When we talked last April, you told me that my path is to be some sort of humanitarian politician and that the work may relate to what I'm currently doing as an acupuncturist. Although I'm a bit of a political hound, I thought this path was funny because so much of that life felt so "not me." I kept mentioning it to people with an "Isn't that funny?" at the end, and everyone said, "Well, I can totally see it."

You also told me that I had to attend or would attend the Democratic National Convention in Denver. At the time I thought I'd have to get there as a national delegate, which wasn't in the cards for me. About two weeks after I spoke to you, I got a call from an organization called Healthcare United, asking me to complete a phone survey. For some reason I said yes, and at the end of the survey the caller asked if I would like to volunteer with their organization. Out of curiosity I said yes, attended their Colorado chapter meeting, and ended up on the Democratic National Convention committee.

Well, Healthcare United sponsored a Healthcare Day parade in Denver during the DNC, and I was there giving free treatments in the free clinic tent, and I got to meet several bigwigs from the Democratic Party. I gave them copies of my personal health care policy statement on the importance of providing alternative treatments as a first step in health care rather than a last resort. It explained the cost benefits compared to more invasive and drug-dependent options and the conditions it would most successfully treat.

Well, I stirred up a lot of important conversations, and I'm getting more and more involved in the political arena. I'm still seeing individual clients, but other avenues for income within the political arena are opening up for me. I'm filled with gratitude and have never felt happier or more alive. I have no idea what's next, but I'm starting to see the path that lies before me.

TO SUMMARIZE THIS CHAPTER

◆ When you chose a birth-path vibration to come in with for a lifetime, that birth path carried a set of core values with it. For example, if you're on the path of the number 1, you will value independence and autonomy, no matter what you do, where you work, or how much you change.

◆ You have other values that change throughout the lifetime as you have new experiences and relationships. Those changing values can lead you to your next career step. For example, you may once have valued adventure and now value helping people. Understanding this shift can help you decide to become a teacher or start a nonprofit foundation.

◆ It's important to examine if your current job reflects your top three values. List the three things you value most today in your career:

1.

2.

3.

- How well does your current job line up with your values?

- Whom would you most like to help in your work?

- How can these insights help you tweak your career?

PART
3

USING YOUR
LIFE FUEL

13

PAIN IS ON PURPOSE; IT REVEALS YOUR MISSION

EVERYTHING THAT HAS HAPPENED to you has been on purpose. You called up the wonderful and terrible players in your drama and perfectly designed your good and bad circumstances. Why? To remember who you are, to remember your mission, and to remember your divine power.

Realize that you're not a victim of the bad economy, job market, or your limited job skills. You have your hands on the steering wheel (whether it feels like it or not). Your life is on purpose. You designed it to get where you are. Quit feeling sorry for yourself, blaming, arguing, and being depressed. Take back your power, and start dreaming up something new and better.

Every wound you've experienced, from loss to illness or disappointment, was exactly what you needed (and chose) in order to arrive at this point in your life. It's all perfect! All the struggle was for a purpose, and you chose it. Your choice is how you react to the pain and what you choose to learn from it. It will eventually become your fuel for moving forward.

Suffering wakes us up, reveals our mission, raises our consciousness, and teaches us wisdom. It's impossible to have a lifetime without pain. It's an essential part of the human experience. In fact pain is the most powerful fuel we have for accomplishing our mission.

Consider the possibility that you chose (consciously or unconsciously) every important job you've had in this lifetime because it was healing you. What pain needs healing now? Let that answer guide you to your next career step.

Our work heals us by letting us offer to the world exactly what we need to heal ourselves. Picture a time when you were younger and were struggling with the core issue of your childhood. Perhaps you felt wounded by your siblings, abandoned by your mother, repressed, or punished for speaking your truth.

If a divine being had come to you at that painful moment, wrapped their arms around you, and whispered something empowering, what would they have said?

For example, if you were feeling alone, abandoned or unloved, they might have said: "You are powerful and divine and greater than your circumstances. You're deeply loved and here to do great work in the world—no matter how limited you feel right now. Rise above this pain. Own your beauty and dignity, and move forward fearlessly."

Would that have helped you find your way?

If so, the mission of your work today is to reach out to those who need to hear that same message and say to them, "You are a powerful, divine being who is greater than your circumstances, deeply loved, and here to do great work in the world—no matter how limited you feel right now. Rise above this pain, and own your beauty and dignity. Move forward fearlessly."

Our greatest work offers to the world exactly what we wished had been offered to us when we were in our deepest pain.

You can offer that message in your unique way, whether that means taking photographs that inspire, being a fashion consultant for women who feel unattractive, becoming a therapist, teacher, artist, healer, or career counselor.

Your path and unique talents reveal the flavor and expression of how you'll bring that message to the world. But that underlying message is the core foundation of your work.

The more powerfully your work is aligned with that core message, the more successful your career will be.

TOM'S STORY

Tom was a brilliant thirty-six-year-old successful attorney with a wife and young daughter whom he adored. He had thrived in the intellectual atmosphere of law school, graduated at the top of his class, and immediately got a prestigious job—where he quickly gained respect from his peers. Through lots of hard work and determination, he climbed the ladder of success at his law firm, handling more and more prestigious cases. His future looked bright, everyone told him. Just a few more years and he would make partner.

But Tom was bored and unhappy. The ideals he had passionately pursued in law school, like justice, knowledge, and equality, were not part of his everyday law practice. Most of his time was spent doing tedious paperwork and arguing mundane cases. And he seldom saw his family.

Because he was on the path of the refined, intellectual number 7, higher learning fueled his hungry mind. Changing the world for the better was his mission. But daily courtroom feuding and endless detailed paperwork were not in alignment with his path.

During one of our sessions Tom told me a story about his early years that revealed his core pain—his demanding, brilliant father had constantly criticized Tom's hard work in school.

"Nothing I ever did, as good as it was, was ever good enough for him. I got straight As in school, but he would want to know why I had one A-minus. There was no positive feedback and constant criticism. My mom became an alcoholic, drinking to cope with Dad's pressure for perfection. I just pushed myself harder academically to please him."

As successful as he was in high school, Tom never felt good enough. When I asked him what a divine being might have said to comfort him in those dark moments of insecurity, he said: "To realize that I didn't have to please anyone; that I was good enough just being me, and that perfection wasn't as important as wisdom, compassion, and spiritual understanding."

During his 7 personal year Tom went through a transformational process. To everyone's surprise he quit the law firm. With his wife's full support, they sold their family home and bought an RV. For an entire year, they traveled the country, visiting friends and relatives and camping out in national parks. Tom spent his days enjoying his family, writing about the deeper meaning of life as he saw it, and reading books that inspired him.

By the end of their yearlong adventure, Tom had written a sixty-thousand-word book about spiritual transformation and walking away from a life that doesn't fit. He's now shopping that book around to publishers, and the project is attracting interest.

He's also getting his teaching certificate. Somewhere along his journey Tom realized that teaching history and government to high school kids would allow him to empower others the way he wished he had been empowered as a child.

His brilliance and compassion will make him a gifted teacher, and he's very excited about getting back into the classroom—but this time as the one guiding others to higher knowledge. The contemplative year he spent traveling with his family brought greater intimacy and affection into their family life. "We've given our daughter memories that she'll carry forever. My wife and I are so close now and in complete alignment with what we want our lives to look like."

HERE'S THE PROOF
THAT YOU PREPROGRAMMED
YOUR GREATEST CHALLENGES

When you look at the big picture of your life and see where your 9 years fall, as well as where your two Saturn returnings hit, you'll probably recognize those junctures as painful times from your past.

You may have lost a loved one, been fired, moved to a new city, or had a health crisis. Examining these predestined cycles and seeing how perfectly they line up with your greatest life challenges is very eye-opening. How could you have been the victim of circumstances if that challenge was already evident in your path from the moment you were born?

Think about it. Who designed your life mission? You did. You preprogrammed the challenges that you would bump into. You wouldn't have designed those challenges into your life plan if you knew you couldn't rise above them.

That means you're here to succeed, to rise above the obstacles, to move forward no matter what gets in your way. That was your original intention. Don't back down now. At the end of your lifetime, you're the one who reviews your life and decides if you've lived up to your potential. And, as you may already have realized, your higher self wants you to succeed.

When you find yourself in extremely challenging circumstances, ask why you chose this. Ask what you're supposed to be changing.

What is your greatest pain today? Have you lost someone you love? Have you suffered injustices or been deeply disappointed? That's your fuel to do great work.

When the designer Ralph Lauren was a child, his parents were poor and had trouble making ends meet. As he dreamed of being elegant like Cary Grant or as original as Jimmy Stewart, he struggled with the shame of wearing hand-me-downs—and he was the last in the family to get them.

While still a teenager Lauren found scraps of silk from which he created classy ties, which he sold to Saks and Bloomingdale's. You know the rest of his amazing story.

Today, when he sees someone dressed in his clothes feeling good about themselves, he says he believes he is doing good work in the world. And he is. His work has healed his own childhood shame, while helping millions of others feel confident about how they look. That's a great example of how our pain becomes our fuel. When you read biographies of great people, you'll always find this link between their pain and the fuel to do their work.

The more pain you feel, the more energy you have to launch your new career. See the pain as fuel—not as something that stops you from moving forward.

Say: "I am moving forward powerfully, using my pain as fuel to do work that makes the world a better place."

Here are the common connections between pain and fuel for various birth paths:

A 1 birth path may be damaged by feeling unaccepted and alone in the world. Their great work provides acceptance, connection, and community to others.

A 2 birth path may be hurting from the stings of hypersensitivity—feeling too much and knowing what others are thinking. Their great work offers balm for other people's sensitivities and heals others from the pain of relationships.

A 3 birth path may grow up feeling uninspired, repressed, and stifled in their creativity. Their great work offers joy, creativity, and new ideas to others—empowering others to express themselves.

A 4 birth path feels trapped by the pressures of hard work, drudgery, and not enough play. Their great work teaches others to organize, work hard, and remember to smell the roses.

A 5 birth path may be prevented from experiencing sensual pleasure or freedom in childhood and later push the boundaries of addiction too far. Their great work involves inspiring others to find their sensuality, openness, and sense of adventure, while also teaching them to find their spiritual center so they don't get lost in addictions.

A 6 birth path feels lost in the needs of others, tries to make loved ones happy in an impossible situation, and doesn't have strong self-worth. Their great work uses their gifts to strengthen communities and empower people to see their own value.

A 7 birth path is hurt by the meaninglessness of life and has turned cynical and isolated. Their great work requires that they teach what they know and inspire others to analyze and intuit the greater meanings of life, and seek spiritual perfection.

An 8 birth path has grown up feeling powerless and later misused their power. Their great work empowers others to find financial success and emotional well-being.

A 9 birth path is stung by past disappointments and looking back at all that's been lost. Their great work requires facing the future, embracing the humanitarian needs of the planet, and helping others let go and move on.

An 11 birth path has trouble managing their sensitive, high-strung energy, which overpowers others and leaves them feeling isolated. Their great work requires that they channel this divine energy into the arts or healing and recognize their role as teachers of higher knowledge.

A 22 birth path has worked too hard, tried to fit in, and lost sight of the big picture. Their great work requires loosening the grip on reality, embracing their divine knowledge, and using it to inspire others.

A GUIDED MEDITATION FOR RECOGNIZING AND RELEASING YOUR DEEPEST PAIN

This particular type of meditation helps people who are recovering from grief. When you feel the pain once a day and release it, the pain quits gnawing at you for the remainder of the day. You've made an appointment to feel your grief and release it, so you can move forward.

1. For twenty minutes sit in quiet meditation using mantra or prayer to quiet your mind. When the mind has settled, ask yourself, What image from my life makes me feel like crying when I think about it?

2. Your strongest pain will usually reveal itself easily when you ask that question. You'll get a visual image of the experience that hurt you. Stay with the vision, and let your heart feel that pain—really experience it. Cry it out, if that feels good to you. Give it a few minutes of your attention.

3. When you've stayed with that pain for five minutes, and you've truly felt it, hold your hands in front of your chest with the palms facing up. Take several slow, deep breaths. Imagine putting that pain into your open palms. See the pain pouring out of your chest and into your hands.

4. Raise your hands toward the sky, and offer that pain up and away from you. Set it free. Offer it to God, Buddha, angels, divine beings, or source energy. Move it out of your chest and away from you.

5. Say aloud, "I release my pain to the higher realms and am grateful for the compassion I've gained from this suffering. I'm using it to move forward and do my great work."

In a dream . . .

I'm standing on a beach surrounded by a vast expanse of dark sand as far as I can see. Gulls are squawking in the distance. I'm looking into my father's watery blue eyes. He's animated and young, explaining something to me with more passion than I ever saw in the last years of his life. His brother, my beloved uncle Pete, who died soon after my dad, is standing beside us, laughing.

We're enjoying the vivid openness of the sand and sky and sharing stories, when behind them in the distance, I see a huge tidal wave rolling along the sand toward us—maybe a hundred feet high and towering ominously over the flat landscape. We turn and see another powerful wave rolling directly toward us from the opposite direction. We're standing between these two oncoming waves, and in an instant we realize there's nothing we can do.

I grab their hands. "How will we remember?" I ask, staring into their eyes. "How will we find each other again?"

"Don't worry," answers my uncle Pete. "We always find each other."

He shouts something else, but I can't hear his words through the sound of the crashing waves. I wake up gasping for breath—still feeling their strong hands wrapped around mine—longing for that moment again, hearing their voices in my head, unable to get back to sleep. Do we always find each other again? Isn't that endless longing the tyranny of grief? Or is it simply our limited perspective on time and space?

Grieving clients constantly seek me out. They fill my appointment book. Maybe they sense I can help them find their footing in the midst of swirling waters. Today my client tells me about her partner who recently died. She hasn't been able to move forward and is lost in her depression. She needs to make a living, yet she's drowning in pain. I explain that she's still here because she hasn't accomplished her mission for this lifetime, and her partner is watching, patiently waiting for her to get to it. "You haven't really lost each other," I explain. "It's just a shift of perspective, a different dimension. Nothing is really lost."

As I say this I get chills over my entire body—a sign that I've tuned into something for her. "Do you know that your partner watches you struggle?" I ask her gently.

My client nods. "He wants me to teach," she says through her tears. In that moment I see the spark in her, the life force, rekindling. We both feel it. She laughs softly.

"Let's talk about how to make that happen," I suggest. Months later she writes, "You encouraged me to fulfill the mission for my life, and I'm getting to it. I've woken up."

Later I'm meditating on a new client. I ask if there are messages from the higher realms to help her move forward. In my meditation I see a gentleman, slumped over and kind of embarrassed, slinking up to me. He mumbles, "Well, it wasn't that great when we were married. Tell her I'm sorry. Tell her she doesn't need to be so angry. I see what I did. I'd like to help. There is money. Tell her to go to school."

I write it all down for our session.

Later when I'm working with her, I learn that her husband died and left a trail of sexual and physical abuse in the family. My client is very lost in her pain, grief, and anger. I give her the messages from her departed husband. She is slightly amused that he's slinking around apologizing.

On further discussion she sees that there might be a way to use money from his estate to fund her return to graduate school, so that she can move her career forward to get to her great work—the work that her pain has fueled her to do.

Her biggest shame, which has weighed her down for years, has been that her husband abused the children. She begins to see that this pain is also the fuel that fires her passion to help others. She looks into graduate school and later tells me, "I feel more clearheaded and focused than I have in years. Thank you so much."

Why does pain drown us?

I reflect back on promises I made to my dying husband twenty-five years before—"We'll find each other again," I whispered at his bedside just before his spirit slipped away. Two years later I repeated the same words to my best childhood girlfriend, Crissie, who was dying of leukemia at the age of thirty-two. On the last day I spent with her, a hot August afternoon, we walked on the beach together, reminiscing about our shared childhood memories, and contemplating the meaning of life and death.

"What's the hardest part?" I asked her.

"Seeing it hurt my father," she said through her tears. How those words haunted me for years—that Crissie suffered not only from her disease but from knowing how grief would weigh down her loved ones.

Perhaps the pain of grief is really the pain of remembering our own home, our true nature, our divinity, and wanting to return there. Aren't we simply longing for that divine realm again, where everything and everyone is luminous and connected?

Yet until our work is done, our lifetime mission accomplished, we can't go home. And every moment we spend longing, instead of moving forward with our great work, is wasted time. I'm certainly guilty of that—creating a limbo of pain instead of just moving forward and getting the mission accomplished.

This is our universal challenge, overcoming the "pitiful voice" that stops us all at the door of greatness. It's those wasted days of feeling "useless, not good enough, not strong enough, not smart enough" or saying, "I don't care." It's the days when we lie down and surrender to doubt.

And most of the time when we're lost in our "pitiful self," we look to the wrong sources for comfort. It takes courage to focus on the higher self, the divinity, the unseen realms for guidance, instead of looking to our peers for approval and support.

But by going to our higher self through meditation, prayers, and dreams, we do find our courage again. In fact that's often the most powerful way to reverse a negative cycle. Here's an example:

Recently, after several days of struggling with self-doubt and praying for guidance, I had this dream: I arrive at a lake and see my spiritual teacher standing on the shore. He tells me to walk through a passageway, and I do. I find myself winding through hallways and emerging into a large room, a simple open white space where several people are sitting on cushions.

At the front of the room is a friend who is teaching meditation to the group. She smiles at me and says it's fine that I'm there. I say that I'm tired, very tired. Someone sitting behind me props up my back as I sit to meditate with the group. I feel nurtured being in that space. We meditate together. As I sit there quietly I become aware that the room, the entire space, is filled with golden light, brighter than sunlight, spilling over all of us. It soothes me. I wake up feeling renewed, still seeing the golden light illuminate the room.

TO SUMMARIZE THIS CHAPTER

◆ Your pain is on purpose; it's fuel to do your great work.

◆ When you remember a painful moment from your early years and imagine someone wrapping their arms around

you saying the words you needed to hear to find your
power again, what would they have said to you?

♦ Those words of empowerment reveal the foundation of
your great work and the gifts you have to offer the world.

♦ Studying your nine-year cycles reveals the challenges you
set up for your lifetime; the ultimate intention of your life
plan is success (living up to your great potential).

♦ The energy and wisdom you bring to your preprogrammed
challenges determine if you live up to your great potential
in this lifetime.

14

FEAR IS YOUR POWER

IS FEAR STOPPING YOU? Well, *duh* . . .

Fear is simply energy—lots of it and focused in the wrong direction. We can't live a courageous, fulfilled life until we learn to use fear as a source of motivation rather than a stopping place.

Have you ever considered that everyone here on planet Earth is afraid of something? Even the most successful, powerful, courageous people you know feel fear. But they don't let it stop them. They think of it as energy—something to use as fuel to move forward.

All great athletes, actors, and mountain climbers know that without the fear, there's no energy to work with. You don't make it to the top of Everest without experiencing fear, and you don't give a great stage performance or win an Olympic gold medal if there isn't a rush of energy (also known as fear) inside you.

Life without fear does not exist on planet Earth, and that's on purpose.

Fear is part of the deep negativity—the mud—we came to push through on planet Earth to help us develop inner strength and power.

Now that you're here, don't forget that. Feel the fear, and do it anyway.

The thing you're most afraid of doing is usually the thing you most need to do in order to live up to your path. For example, are you afraid of leaving the security of a monthly paycheck and benefits to launch your own business? Are you afraid of opening your heart totally and trusting another person with your feelings? Are you afraid of going back to school? Are you afraid of teaching what you know because you think someone will doubt your abilities?

Take a hard look at those fears. Your gift to the world and to yourself is hiding behind those doorways. Walk through the fear, and you won't look back with regret.

"But what if I fail?" you may ask.

Fear of failure is simply *fear*. And fear is at the low end of your energy continuum. It's your negativity. Whenever you operate from fear of failure, things don't turn out well. You actually attract negativity into your life with that fear. Change your energy, and operate from optimism and inspiration. It's the only way to attract success.

Imagine you're at the end of your life. You're reviewing what you've accomplished and didn't accomplish in this lifetime. Are you happy with your choices? Have you lived up to your full potential? Have you made a difference in the world with your gifts? Did you overcome the challenges you preset in your path before the lifetime began? Did you love those around you fearlessly enough? Your answers to these questions will help you overcome your fear and move forward on the path you came here to fulfill.

If you have children, please understand that they learn how to make choices in life from watching what you do—rather than listening to what you say. Are you modeling a life of fear-based choices? Do you want them to have a better life than you did? Teach them to live fearlessly, to make courageous choices. And the only way to teach that lesson is to live it.

ELLEN'S STORY

Ellen, who owned an adventure travel company, had traveled the world from the time she was in her mother's womb; her father was Greek and had worked in the shipping industry. In college, she had majored in anthropology to pursue her love of exotic cultures. She later earned a master's degree in counseling so she could use her brilliant mind to help people.

She was on the master soul path of the 22/4. (The sum of her birth date numbers was 22, whichever way it was added. This meant that she chose to live up to her lifetime mission from the very beginning without the possibility of avoiding her great work.)

Ellen had wrapped her powerful 22 path with Virgo, which meant that her analytical mind would be her gift and challenge as she learned to focus on solutions rather than the imperfections of life.

As I prepped for our first session, I saw that she'd had a very intense and often painful life. There had been devastating losses designed to kick her firmly on path, as well as many rich opportunities. I could see that she worked hard, harder than anyone else in the travel company she owned, and that she was exhausted.

It was clear that one of her challenges was her tendency to get lost in the drudgery of hard work. I would have to help her remember to focus on the bigger picture and accomplish the great work of the 22 path— inspiring the world with new ideas and ways of living.

She was in a 9 personal year and moving into her second Saturn returning. It was major life-reinvention time, and I was excited to be working with her.

During our first session Ellen told me that while she was a graduate student at an Ivy League school, she had fallen in love with Phillip, a brilliant professor who traveled the world interviewing people for an unusual research project. She accompanied Phillip on these trips, conducting psychological research and helping him interview and write the stories.

As Ellen and Phillip traveled the world conducting research, their relationship deepened into a romantic one, and they had a child together; their lives were now intertwined through love, family, work, and an intellectual hunger for the deeper meaning of life.

Tragically, while returning home from a trip, Phillip was killed in a plane crash.

"It felt like someone had punched me in the gut, and I couldn't catch my breath for a long, long time," she explained. "I went into survival mode." Ellen felt she couldn't continue the work without Phillip, and now she had a child to raise.

Falling back on what she knew best, she launched a travel company. Yet the travel business was exhausting, and she felt empty inside.

Since she was currently in a 9 personal year, it was time to grieve and release the pain of Phillip's death so she could move on. Her looming Saturn returning meant there was no choice but to step up to the great work waiting inside her—to educate and inspire the world with new thoughts. As we processed her pain and talents, we saw more clearly what that great work looked like and how to maneuver her life to create it.

"What would Phillip say about the work you're doing now—the travel business?" I asked her.

"Well, he would be proud of me for doing something on my own. But he'd be a little annoyed with me for avoiding the real work, for not carrying on with what we started together. I've known he was annoyed with me for a while, through my dreams. I just don't know how to do the other work without him," she explained.

We made a list of baby steps she could take to navigate this reinvention.

A few months later I heard from her again. "I'm very afraid of moving forward," she admitted tearfully. "I'm a single mom, and what if I fail? And I'm not sure I'm ready to come out of the closet about what I believe

in—to pursue the work that Phillip and I did without him. I always hid be-
hind him and his success."

"If you didn't have that fear, I'd be worried," I explained. "Feel it and
use it to get you out of your routine, out of your drudgery, and away from
your grief."

Ellen wanted her son to see that you can be very afraid but pick your-
self up and find your courage again. "That would be the greatest legacy
I could leave him."

When we last spoke, she was leaving for Brazil to speak at a confer-
ence that would allow her to tell the story of the work she and Phillip had
done together and what she had learned from it. By delegating many of
her responsibilities from the travel company to a trusted business man-
ager, she had freed up her schedule. She was in negotiations with a pub-
lishing agent discussing the book she was writing about her work with
Phillip. She felt it was the beginning of her new, more authentic direction.

TO SUMMARIZE THIS CHAPTER

◆ Fear is simply energy—which we can harness and use to
   move forward.

◆ Fear is present in everyone no matter how a person's life
   looks from the outside.

◆ When we're faced with an important career choice, our
   fear shows us the choice we should make. It shows us what
   we should do to live up to our potential.

◆ Teaching your children to move beyond fear can help them
   live up to their own potential.

PART
4

TAPPING INTO YOUR
OWN INTUITIVE
CAREER GUIDANCE

15

YOUR INNER GPS SYSTEM

IT SOMETIMES TAKES A challenging circumstance or a great loss to get us to examine our lives deeply. Yet no one gets through a lifetime (and shouldn't) without bumping up against those great questions: Why am I here? What did I come here to do?

Yes, your life *is* on purpose. All the pain and joy, suffering and glory that you've experienced have been to get you to this moment so that you can use every experience as fuel for what you came here to do.

Aligning your work with the mission you originally intended to accomplish in this lifetime requires tapping into your higher guidance and listening to your intuition. That's where your inner GPS system is pulsing out the directions you need to move forward. That road map can only be found inside you—and nowhere else.

Without understanding that each answer you need is already available to you, you're at the mercy of every passing opinion or criticism of your life—which will certainly throw you off course. Tapping in requires sitting still and shutting up at least once a day.

Here's how to tap into your higher guidance:

SHUT UP!

Learn to stop the constant chatter of your mind that fills your head with fear and negative beliefs about what's possible for you. The most powerful and time-tested way to do this is through prayer, meditation, or chanting. There's a science to creating alpha brain waves—the quiet place where chatter ceases.

Many spiritual traditions have this formula figured out. Whether you choose to repeat a prayer such as the Our Father, a mantra (a sacred word or phrase, such as Om namah Shivaya—which means "I bow to the divine self"), or to follow your breath, you will begin to experience the consciousness inside you that is separate from and greater than your mind. You are not your thoughts. You're a great, wise, and powerful energetic being connected to the divine fabric that entangles us to all other energetic beings in the universe.

Find at least ten minutes a day to practice quieting your mind. If you're an athlete, pray or repeat a mantra while running, biking, riding, hiking, or swimming. You'll notice a higher vibration frequency than normal after your workout. And yes, quieting the mind does create endorphins—the feel-good hormones. But, most important, it opens up a space for your guidance to come through loud and clear.

How do I know this? In the early eighties, after my husband died, I was taught transcendental meditation. This well-known meditation technique improves brain wave patterns, revitalizes energy, enhances concentration, and generally makes you a happier, more peaceful person.

Since then my meditation technique has evolved with guidance from several highly advanced spiritual teachers including Sri Shambhavananda, at the Eldorado Mountain Ashram in Colorado, who descends from the line of spiritual teachers identified with the late Guru Muktananda from India. I've spent plenty of time studying in ashrams and had ancient knowledge passed down to me through these teachers. I still meditate at least twice a day and am deeply grateful for and to the teachers who shared their powerful knowledge with me.

Daily meditation has had a profoundly positive effect on the quality of my life, as well as my ability to tap into intuition. If you choose to do only one thing from this book to improve your life, find a meditation teacher and incorporate meditation into your daily life. It will enable you greater access to your inner guidance system—also known as intuition.

STATE YOUR REQUEST

Human lifetimes center on freedom of choice; our guides (whether they're our departed loved ones, angels, or enlightened masters) aren't allowed to interfere in our lives without an invitation. They must wait until we make a request, and then they're required to help. (It's their job.) At the end of your daily meditation or prayer, say or write, "Show me the path I came in to manifest for my highest good. I'm ready to move forward."

Keep repeating those words until you feel a response inside you. If the answer you receive feels good, even makes you giggle, it's probably advice from a higher being who has your best interests at heart. Listen to it and act accordingly. If you continually ignore what your guides tell you, they'll step back and wait until you're more open.

Whenever you doubt you'll find your true work, say, "I am being guided to use my gifts and talents with all of my passion to make the world a better place in my unique way." When contemplating a new career, examine if the new work is in alignment with this statement. If so, go after it.

PRACTICE EVERY DAY

Get into the practice of pausing and asking for intuitive guidance before making an important phone call, going to a meeting, or making a big decision. When you start listening to your higher self, things will go more smoothly in your life. Many of our struggles are caused by forging ahead to do things our way, no matter what our gut tells us. We can work smarter and more gracefully by first taking time to pause and ask for guidance—especially before applying for a job, asking for a raise, or launching a new business.

By the way, you didn't sign up for this lifetime to go it alone. You knew you had a team of higher beings who would help guide you along the way. It's time to remember that and make good use of that higher guidance, so that you *will* fulfill the destiny you came here to achieve.

INCREASE YOUR FREQUENCY IN ORDER TO CONNECT

When we're pulsing out a low vibration (because of fatigue, negative thoughts, or negative feelings), we're not capable of connecting with the higher self, our divine guides, or the higher knowledge. Connecting is a two-way process; we must increase our vibration while our guides lower theirs, in order to get on the same frequency.

How do we raise our energy? Prayer (especially the Lord's Prayer), chanting, meditation, openhearted laughter, gratitude, and sweetness all increase our frequency level. We can also raise our energy by shifting the focus of our thoughts away from what's troubling us to what we would prefer. That simple shift of focus helps immediately.

Inspiring music, art, and physical endeavors can also shift us to a higher frequency. Dreaming of what we want to happen (especially when it makes us giggle) is another great way to speed up frequency.

No matter how desperate you feel, shift out of your fear and negativity when you ask for help. It's the only way to access higher knowledge.

In the next chapter I'll teach you my favorite way of increasing frequency in order to connect with divine guidance.

TO SUMMARIZE THIS CHAPTER

◆ Stop the negative chatter in your mind through prayer, meditation, or chanting. These are time-tested methods for raising your energy and tapping into your higher guidance.

◆ State your request to the universe. Say: "Show me the path I came in to manifest for my highest good. I'm ready to move forward."

◆ Throughout the day, say: "I am being guided to use my gifts and talents to make the world a better place in my unique way."

◆ Before making decisions about your career, tap into your higher guidance and wait for an answer. When the mind is quiet, you'll get your answer.

16

TUNING UP YOUR VIBES

You may have signed up for great opportunities this time around—as well as significant challenges. You may have made powerful soul agreements with your loved ones to cause you pain and pleasure—simply to help you remember who you are and what you came to do. Nevertheless you're in charge of how your life unfolds.

Will you rise above those heartbreaking events to see the divine order in everything and everyone? Will you see how your pain fuels your great work in the world? Or will you wallow in the "pitiful self" complaining about the challenges that you set up for yourself? This is, of course, the universal human challenge.

Once we get here and marinate in negative human beliefs and thoughts, we forget that we programmed it all ourselves, for better or worse. And we forget that we're in charge of our own success or failure.

How does this happen? Well, think of it this way. We wouldn't come here to planet Earth if it didn't provide the proper training ground for our development. If it weren't for the deep challenges of negativity that exist on the human plane, which are beautifully designed to push us into our wisdom and power, we wouldn't go through the effort of living this out.

If you're a great athlete training for the Olympics and dreaming of a gold medal, wouldn't you find the best training facility and the best coach to push you past your limits so you could succeed? Think of planet Earth as one big Olympic training facility with the best coaches possible to help you succeed.

When it gets challenging don't sit around complaining and crying about it. (Okay, maybe you can do that for a little while after you fall off the balance beam.) But it's all about getting back up, wiping away the tears, and trying again. That attitude is what makes the human spirit so inspiring. You have powerful inner strength and resiliency inside you. Use it.

Our human challenge is simply to live each day courageously and turn around each little setback. We use our thoughts, beliefs, and feelings to do that.

All of us have a million reasons to feel bad at any given moment during our day. Circumstances change for the better and for the worse in a constant flow of events. We react to those circumstances as we've been taught to by our families, teachers, and friends. We believe we have little choice in how we react. And even if we did react in a different way, what would it matter? This is truly the "human condition."

Scientists and spiritual teachers alike have aligned themselves behind one idea—everything is energy. Everything you see, sit on, feel—the sun on your face, children's laughter, a good run, prayer, a great kiss—is all source energy: what everything and everyone came from.

You're composed of this same energy—and its frequency can be raised or lowered according to your thoughts, feelings, and beliefs. The frequency you send out at any given time attracts like frequencies. Like attracts like.

For example, when you're feeling joy and gratitude, your vibration puts you on a plane where you can connect with and attract other elements that vibrate on the higher plane. Thus you can bring wonderful things into your life when you're feeling good. (Haven't you noticed this is true? When you're having a great day, wonderful things happen to you all day long. When you're having a bad day, things seem to get worse and worse, don't they?)

Here's the surprise: These ups and downs are because of *your* energy—not because of external forces working on you. Each of us has an energy continuum—negative at the bottom, positive at the top. Positive energy includes our brilliance, goodness, divinity, inspiration, love, passion, optimism, happiness, and joy (our connectedness).

Negative energy includes our anger, depression, sadness, guilt, pessimism, meanness, sense of lack, drudgery, and separateness—not only from others but also from our source energy.

Everyday we bounce up and down on this continuum, reacting to our circumstances. We feel that if only our circumstances would change, we could be happy. The ultimate irony is that if we get happy, our circumstances will change to meet us.

Moving up your energy continuum (in spite of circumstances) by changing your energy to a higher frequency and opening up to source energy connects you to inspiration, spirituality, and goodness. It changes your life for the better.

Imagine your energy continuum as a fuel gauge. When the fuel tank in your car nears empty, you worry about running out of gas and being stranded—which is separateness and stagnation. When it's full you're confident and able to explore. You have unlimited energy and ideas—which means inspiration and productivity.

You're in control of what level you vibrate on, thus you're in control of what happens to you on any given day. Your emotions determine what level you're vibrating on. When you feel love and joy, you're at the highest level attracting the most wonderful things into your life. When you're feeling despair, you attract more of the same.

No matter how positive your energy is, you will still have challenging events. We sign up for those (karmas) in order to learn and grow. However, your reaction to those events determines their outcome. Your energy level determines whether you react well or poorly to a crisis and how your life unfolds from there. A good life requires good energy. It's that simple.

LEARN ENERGETIC PERSONAL RESUSCITATION—EPR

My favorite technique for quickly raising energy to a higher vibration is what I call energetic personal resuscitation (EPR). EPR is a quick, easy technique for switching energy to a higher frequency. These three quick emergency switches are humor, gratitude, and sweetness.

You can use these three energy-saving techniques quickly and effectively in any emergency situation where your energy is at the low end of your continuum. By switching to one of these feelings, you'll rise higher on your continuum and thus be better able to respond to the crisis.

HUMOR: This is a very quick way to easily tap into source energy. When we laugh with big, openhearted, unrestrained laughter, we're recognizing the absurdity of life. We start to see the big picture. We start connecting to our higher selves and our inner guidance system.

GRATITUDE: This is the most powerful high-vibration feeling we can tap into. When you get it pulsing through you, you'll feel opened up and receptive to source energy. Gratitude works especially well to counteract anger. By sending this high-level emotion to someone you have conflict with, the conflict will begin to soften. You will no longer be a victim in this relationship.

SWEETNESS: When we show our true sweet authentic selves to others, they open up and show us their sweetness. It's like holding a baby. We see the sweetness and go there to join it. If we switch to sweetness in the midst of conflict, we'll see instant positive results and a better resolution.

Try using EPR in a tight situation. If you're standing in line at the post office and the long wait is driving you crazy, use EPR to improve your energy—which will instantly improve the situation. As you experiment with your ability to shift energy in everyday circumstances, you'll see how powerful you are. When you bump up against one of your predestined lifetime challenges, shifting to higher energy will be second nature.

Try to remember a time when you successfully improved a difficult situation by using EPR. Make a habit of using EPR every day when you would normally react to a situation with anger, fear, or other forms of negativity. Keep note of how EPR affects your life. Experiment with it next time you're in a difficult meeting or dealing with an angry loved one. It's a powerful tool for raising your vibrations and helping you connect with your inner guidance.

TO SUMMARIZE THIS CHAPTER

◆ When you chose to have a human lifetime, you knew it would be a great challenge, but you signed up anyway. You wanted to push against the negativity and learn to use your energy to make things better—because this would help you evolve to your highest potential.

◆ You can easily shift your energy from negative to positive by using energetic personal resuscitation (EPR): humor, gratitude, and sweetness. These three emotions quickly raise our energy so we can improve our circumstances and tap into our higher selves.

◆ Everyday situations provide great energy-training opportunities. Practice improving life's little frustrations by quickly shifting your energy from negative to positive. This will strengthen your energy mastery skills so that when a big challenge hits, it's second nature to shift to positive energy and influence circumstances for the better.

◆ This EPR energy-shifting technique will help you tap into your intuitive guidance, find your true work, and make it successful—against all odds.

17

STOP THE
PITIFUL THINKING

IMAGINE THAT YOU SIGNED up for every painful challenge you've had in your life with the intention of rising above it and evolving in the way your spirit needed to. Imagine that you signed up for this because you knew that as you raised your consciousness, you would help hundreds and thousands of people around you evolve, since we're all in this dance together.

Or, as the quantum physicists say, we're all made from the same energy membrane. We're part of the vast energetic fabric that makes up our universe; a positive ripple in one piece of the fabric affects the entire membrane. Translation: *You* are responsible for evolving to your full potential so that your higher vibration affects millions of the rest of us.

Maybe you became stuck in a negative-thinking loop such as, "I'll never find a career that makes me happy and abundant at the same time." Now imagine that each time you focused on this thought, you gave it more energy.

And what if that thought made your negative reality more and more true for you? Not only for you, but for everyone around you?

Imagine if those fear-based thoughts helped create a negative community of people stuck in negative thinking. Everywhere you went you would hear those negative thoughts come bouncing back to you from your loved ones, family, and friends. Then you could say, "See, everyone knows that life is miserable and pointless."

Do you see how powerful you are? For better or worse, you're the master here.

Our thoughts are pure energy, as is everything else in our universe. When you think a thought you're actually sending out a vibrational message that everyone and everything around you reacts to unconsciously.

If it's a positive thought about something you want to happen, your thought energy begins rearranging subatomic particles to make that event happen.

If it's a negative thought about something you're afraid of, your fear acts like a beacon attracting exactly what you don't want.

Your fear voice tells you all the reasons why you can't do what you want to do for a living. You might think that's being "practical" or "realistic." It's not. It's your "pitiful self" abusing your powerful self. Choose to be your brilliant, powerful, fearless divine self. The world will align itself with your dreams.

As human beings addicted to pitiful thinking, we spend way too much time mulling over our problems. We focus on what's wrong with our lives, thinking that somehow this will make things better. It's a law of quantum physics that what we focus on gets bigger. (See the appendix for more on this subject.)

Simply by becoming aware of what we're thinking about and switching the mind to focus on solutions, we can solve our "impossible" problems. Remember, your thoughts are energy. Send your focused energy to what you want to happen, not to what you fear.

When you find yourself stuck in your negative thought loop, pull out of it as if you're a pilot pulling your plane out of dive. Do anything to raise your energy to a higher vibration such as the humor, sweetness, and gratitude techniques (energetic personal resuscitation) described in chapter 16.

Try using those positive affirmations that you read about everywhere. They actually do work. For example, maybe your negative thought is: The economy is terrible, and I'll never succeed at starting my own business.

How do you feel when you say this?

Defeated? Well, then you are!

Try this thought instead: When I raise my energy and live true to my authentic mission, I attract enormous opportunities that I can't even begin to imagine now.

NEGATIVE BELIEFS AND POSITIVE ANTIDOTES

Aside from what you're thinking about today, you probably have a slew of lifetime beliefs that you carry around silently inside you. These are beliefs (or stories) about how you think life works. For example, maybe you tell yourself, There are good people and bad people in the world, and they never change.

Wow, what a depressing view of human evolution that says no one ever grows from their experiences or lives up to their great potential unless they start out fabulous from day one! If you truly believed this, do you think you would ever try to genuinely help people or speak honestly to them to help them grow? Would you believe in and be inspired by the beauty of the human spirit? I don't think so.

Your lifetime vibration would sink into depression, and unless you changed that negative belief, you would probably never live up to your own potential. If people can't change, then neither can you. Right?

Try this negative belief: We're all just here to get by and collect our paychecks and benefits. That's the best we can hope for.

Believe it or not, many people believe that. They have jobs they hate, and they think it's pointless or impossible to change careers. Their anger at and hatred of their own condition seep out and poison everyone around them—from family members to people in their community.

These unempowering negative beliefs are at the core of all of our problems, from chronic depression to health challenges, rotten marriages, and jobs that go nowhere. And these tormenting beliefs usually go insidiously undiscovered, since we don't go around announcing proudly that we think this way. Instead they're the quiet, undermining forces in our lives.

It's enormously important to dig up these quiet toxic beliefs and recognize how they're creating your reality. When you think, Well, it doesn't matter how hard I work, I never get recognition, and I'm never seen for who I really am, the universal source feels that low-end vibration belief and provides you abundantly with more of the same negative energy (and negative circumstances) to match what you're sending out.

The first step is recognizing your quiet, unspoken, negative beliefs.

The tricky thing about this is that we live in a very negatively oriented world. If you listen to conversations around you, or watch the news, you'll notice that most discussions have a negative focus. Things are grim and getting grimmer, according to just about everybody. So why would you question these beliefs?

You accept a very limited view of life's possibilities when you accept this group consciousness of negativity and the beliefs that go along with it, such as: There's never enough money; life is very hard; nobody gets a great life unless they're selfish; everyone gets sick. Think this way and you will have a very limited life—with very little chance of living up to the great potential you already outlined for yourself in this lifetime. It's your choice. What you believe is what you get.

Become an observer of the mind. Whenever you hear a negative belief cross your mind, turn it around. Think instead: When I raise my energy, I attract everything I want and need, and I raise the vibration of the planet, which helps other people.

Just by thinking of something that makes you feel joy or gratitude and makes you vibrate at a higher level, you're aligning yourself with forces that bring joy and happiness into your life. This is the power of affirmations; they change your feelings—which change your world.

While doing the exercises in this book that help you identify your destined career path, you must also raise your vibrations (by feeling joy, love, divinity, inspiration, etc.) so that you can attract higher guidance as well as new opportunities into your life.

Your first question each morning should be: Where am I on my energy continuum, and how can I raise my energy just a few notches?

MARY'S STORY

Mary sat cross-legged in her chair, arms crossed, staring me down. "I started to pursue this new line of work that we've come up with, but I became paralyzed," she explained to me. "Every time I tried to pick up the phone to do the networking calls you suggested, a voice inside me said, You're crazy. You fail at everything. You're inept. Don't waste your time on this. Just go get a minimum-wage job. Get security. You'll fail at this new stuff. Who do you think you are, anyway?"

It was my second session with Mary, a thirty-five-year-old single mom who had been an administrative assistant for fifteen years. Mary was on the path of the number 2 with the sun sign of Cancer wrapped around her path. Her heightened sensitivity was at once her gift and her downfall. At every pivotal turning point in her life she had let the doubts that others had about her abilities stop her from moving forward.

Yet she was here to support others in bigger ways than just focusing on the mundane everyday details of organization and paperwork, and she knew that. At her highest potential she could be teaching or counseling and using her gift of sensitivity to help others.

She shared her dream of starting a nonprofit foundation where she could help single moms get legal and financial support to improve their lives. She pictured herself being like a "nurturing grandmother" to these women in transition, providing them with services and support and receiving joy and gratitude in return. This was certainly in alignment with her life mission.

In our first session we had come up with a plan to help her move forward in baby steps. Yet the self-doubt was already stopping her. We spent a few sessions teaching her how to focus her thoughts and feelings on what she wanted to happen rather than what she feared. I taught her to quiet her mind with prayer and meditation, so she could tap into her higher self. She visualized her perfect future at the end of her morning meditation.

We discussed how listening to the fear voice inside her head gave it energy and made it get more powerful. "The more often you ignore it, thank it for the input, and then go about doing your work anyway, the weaker that voice will get," I explained. "Humor is a great antidote to fear. Whenever you hear the fear voice, give a great big laugh out loud, and it will begin to go away."

Her homework list of baby steps included getting informational and networking interviews lined up with three social services employees in order to learn more about changing her career in that direction.

She showed up for her next appointment with a huge smile on her face and leaned back in her chair looking calm and at ease. "I've done it," she said, grinning. "I've got five interviews lined up. The first time that voice really tried to stop me, and I just laughed at it. It's so familiar to me. It's like an old friend. So I laughed at it and picked up the phone and made the call anyway. I got the interview! Then I started feeling cocky and wanted to see how many interviews I could line up—more than we expected. It went beautifully. By the time I made my last call, the little fear voice was barely a whisper and very easy to ignore."

Mary eventually found a job in social services doing intake interviews with clients. She felt needed and appreciated, and she knew she was doing something more in alignment with her life mission. It was a huge improvement for her self-esteem.

Meanwhile she enrolled in an adult college offering evening classes toward getting her master's degree in social work. As of now this single mom with three kids is supporting her family by working at a job that has meaning for her and is enjoying the evening classes that are taking her career in a better direction. She has also begun networking with nonprofit experts and creating the business plan that will help start her own nonprofit. More doors are opening for her every day as she makes career choices that are in alignment with her path.

TO SUMMARIZE THIS CHAPTER

- ◆ Our thoughts are pure energy. When you think a thought you're actually sending out a vibrational message that everyone and everything around you reacts to unconsciously.

- ◆ We spend way too much time focusing on what's wrong with our lives, thinking that somehow this will make things better. It's a law of quantum physics that what we focus on gets bigger.

- ◆ You probably have a slew of negative beliefs about how the world works that you silently carry around inside you.

These unempowering negative beliefs are at the core of all problems—from chronic depression to health challenges, rotten marriages, and jobs that go nowhere.

♦ These tormenting beliefs usually go insidiously undiscovered, since we don't go around announcing proudly that we think this way. Instead they're the quiet, undermining forces in our lives.

♦ Become an observer of the mind. Whenever you hear a negative belief cross your mind, turn it around. Think instead: When I raise my energy, I attract everything I want and need, and I raise the vibration of the planet, which helps many others.

♦ While doing the exercises in this book that help you identify your destined career path, you must also raise your vibrations (by feeling joy, love, divinity, inspiration, and the like) so that you can attract higher guidance as well as new career opportunities into your life.

18

YOUR DREAMS
ARE BY DESIGN

B Y NOW YOU UNDERSTAND the challenges and opportunities
you've signed up for in this lifetime, as well as the energetic influences you're working with.

You *will* have challenging circumstances—people you love will die,
you may go through financial hardships, and you may have health
problems. Those things are part of the fabric of our shared human experience.

Stop wasting time complaining about what you signed up for,
and use your power for good by using your thoughts, feelings, and
dreams to make life go in a more positive direction—even as you
grieve the loss of a loved one or heal yourself from illness.

You came here to live up to your highest potential and overcome
every challenge. You have all the tools inside you to do that. Shift
your focus from the problem to the solution. And never forget how
powerful your mind is.

Your thoughts are pure, focused energy that have a positive or
negative impact on everyone and everything in your life. One of the

greatest ways to focus that pure energy and create positive outcomes is to dream.

We're told from the time we're children to stop dreaming, to get our heads out of the clouds, and to face reality. Yet dreaming helps create our reality. Dreams make us happy and attract better circumstances and relationships into our lives.

WHAT DO YOU DREAM ABOUT?

Play the five-million-dollar game. You suddenly have five million dollars in your bank account, perfect health, and perfect relationships. Feel the ease in your life. From that place of ease and fun, imagine the vacation you would take. Picture it. Feel the deep relaxation of your new life.

You're back home from your vacation, and the universe tells you that you can only keep this abundant wealth if you use it to take your career to the next level and launch your true work—the work you came here to do. What would you do?

What career choices will you make when you aren't limited by money? Will you start a business, create a nonprofit foundation, go back to school, write a book? Now you're starting to think out of the box.

This kind of dreaming loosens up the mind to explore new ideas rather than run the same thought loops you've been running for years. It also opens you up to your intuitive guidance—your inner GPS system. Spend ten minutes tonight asking yourself these questions:

What would make me happy right now? What would make me happy this week? What do I want to happen in the next six months? Where do I want my life to be one year from today? Five years from today? If the answers make you giggle, you have it right.

The question is *not*: What work can I do?

The question *is*: What work did I come here to do that I'd love doing?

DREAMY CAREERS

Now that your mind is open to new possibilities and your own inner guidance, contemplate the career ideas that have been popping up in your consciousness for years. They can be silly or serious. You should have at least ten of these dreamy careers on your list. And the important question is: Do I feel happy and excited when I imagine myself doing this work every day?

To help you get started on your list, here are some ideas in alignment with your birth path.

A 1 birth path wants to be a consultant and teach leadership.

A 2 birth path has often imagined being a therapist or intuitive.

A 3 birth path longs to dance, write, design, and creatively self-express.

A 4 birth path wants to build something from scratch.

A 5 birth path dreams of being a travel guide.

A 6 birth path would love to be a healer.

A 7 birth path has a book to write and wants to go back to school.

An 8 birth path dreams of retiring as a millionaire.

A 9 birth path sees herself teaching the global community.

An 11 birth path dreams of creating inspired music, art, and relationships.

A 22 birth path longs to teach the world a new way of living.

When you've made your list of dreamy careers, slowly go down your list, putting your hand over each career. Pause for a moment and feel the energy in your body while you picture working at each career. Do you feel inspired and giggly when you pause over this career and sense the energy of it? Or do you feel tired, bored, and filled with drudgery? This is a powerful way to tap into your inner career guidance. Your feelings will give you a true read on which career is the right next step. Trust your gut!

SEE IT FIRST

When we dream and imagine what we want to happen, we tap into source energy, intuitive guidance, and our inner GPS system. We tap into the boundless realm of ever-changing possibilities rather than our limited view of fixed outcomes, which is all we can see from the bottom end of our energy continuum.

When you read the list of birth-path-based careers or made your own list of dreamy careers, did you hear those little voices inside your head saying, You'll never be able to do that because of . . . ? Of course you did. That's our human condition. But there is hope!

By changing our negative beliefs about what's possible and opening ourselves instead to positive outcomes from our challenges, we set the energy in place to make what we want happen.

Before going to the job interview that "you know you won't get" or before asking a banker for a new business loan, take a moment and see the interaction going beautifully with everyone—especially you—operating from his or her high end.

See the banker saying, "Yes, I think we can put something together to help you launch your business." See the company CEO saying, "We're always looking for people like you. When can you start?"

See lots of laughter and good feeling in the room. Feel how happy you'll be after the meeting.

Consider the possibility that if you spent even a couple of minutes each day seeing positive outcomes for all your worries, your life would go in a better direction. Isn't it worth a little experimenting?

Consider how much time you currently spend imagining worse-case scenarios. Realize that each second you spend imagining those scenarios you're actually attracting negative energy into your life.

If you really understood how powerful you are, and how you influence your reality with thoughts, dreams, and beliefs, your life would instantly improve. By not accepting responsibility for the effect your energy has on the circumstances of your life, you remain a victim.

Victims hate their jobs, can't find better ones, can't launch their own businesses, are often sick, and seldom have enough money. Are you a victim?

First ask yourself, What do I really want? Then see it happening. Those two steps are enough to change your life dramatically.

WHAT DO YOU BELIEVE?

Let's say that you know what your great work looks like, you've remembered what you came here to do, and yet you're paralyzed about taking the first step to make it happen. Don't worry; this happens.

It's those quiet, long-held, and terribly damaging negative beliefs that are stopping you.

For example, have you ever thought, Who do I think I am to want great success and abundant money? Do you believe that few people ever get true success or happiness—and you're not worthy of being one of them? Have you ever succeeded at something big and then questioned if you were worthy of that achievement?

Our biggest fear is usually the fear of how powerful and magnificent we really are. It's terrifying to believe in our greatness. It goes against every message we've been taught our whole lives. If we follow the belief system we've been raised with—that humans are limited beings with limited capacity for happiness—we settle for a "normal" life and limited amounts of *everything*.

Ask yourself this question: Who is more capable of doing great work to help the suffering people of our world—someone who's on path, doing their true work, and has manifested great wealth that they can use to start a school for girls in Africa? Or someone who struggles to pay the rent and can barely provide for themselves?

The more success and abundance we attract, the more we can use that to do good work in the world. Along with abundance comes a responsibility to help others. If we don't step up to that responsibility, we lose our purpose and meaning.

Imagine if you truly recognized that you're an energy being with unlimited potential for creation, inspiration, divinity, and happiness. Your world would be completely different from the one you live in today. Dare yourself to break out of this low-level social consciousness that governs most of our lives. If you don't believe it—you can't have it. Just say *yes*!

THE ENERGY OF MONEY

When you're living true to your authentic mission, doing your great work, remembering who you came here to be, the money follows. It's part of our divine plan. Why would you set up a lifetime with a mission of doing a particular kind of work to raise the vibration of the planet and then get here and not be able to make a living doing that work? You wouldn't set that up for yourself: It's against the laws of divine order.

Yet our culture tells us that we'll only make money if we follow career paths that, in the past, have lead others to financial success. In other words, be practical and face reality. Behave like everyone else. Believing this will prevent you from following your own inner guidance to the mission you came to accomplish. And being off path will cause unhappiness and fear, which block your ability to attract abundant money.

Consider the possibility that—as the physicists say—money is simply energy. And maybe it's your fear around money that's stopping you from manifesting your true work and having financial abundance.

Can you imagine yourself wealthy and living a life of ease? Can you picture it? That's the first step—believing you can have it and seeing your life with it.

I've worked with hundreds of clients who say, "I hate my job, and I only stay with it to pay the bills." When I ask if they've created financial ease with this job they hate, the answer is always no. They're hardly making ends meet, no matter how big their salary is.

Why? Because money doesn't flow to us when we're off path and stuck in our negative energy. It's impossible for the energy of money to flow through negativity.

Only by following your high-end emotions to find the work you signed up for will you create true financial abundance in your life. If you stay at a job you hate, you might make a reasonable salary and have some savings. But the money will disappear like water running through your fingers.

When you're doing the work you came here to do, feeling empowered and inspired, the money follows. When you hate your work, it hates you back. Like attracts like. Find your great work, and love your life. It's the only recipe for wealth.

THE ENERGY OF HEALTH

The same energetic principles that apply to finding work you love also apply to finding good health. Have you ever had a stress headache or an upset stomach caused by anxiety? Those health problems are obvious results of negative thoughts and beliefs. But how about heart disease and the millions of other illnesses we struggle with?

The journey to health begins with your thoughts and beliefs. You must believe that you can enjoy perfect health, see yourself as perfectly healthy, and live the life you came to live. If you're off path for many years, health issues will surface as your soul tries to wake you up. Just taking that first step toward following your true mission puts you in alignment with perfect health.

Scientific research supports the notion that our happiness is directly connected to our health. Dean Ornish, M.D., author of *Love and Survival: The Scientific Basis for the Healing Power of Intimacy*, found that heart attack patients recovered much faster when they felt loved and nurtured by someone in their community. He also found that the incidence of heart disease was lower in communities where there was a strong sense of connection and caring, both of which are high-end emotions.

Candace Pert, Ph.D., author of *Molecules of Emotion*, researched neuropeptides (chemical messengers in the body) and found that these molecules provide a link between mind and body. In other words, there is scientific proof that our thoughts and emotions affect our health—for better and for worse.

That is why we need to ask ourselves, What did I come here to do?

If we're not working true to our mission, we're not marinating in our joy and inner peace. We're spending too much time immersed in the negative emotions of depression, pessimism, anger, and anxiety.

Marinating in those negative emotions will cause illnesses. Our only pathway back to health will be to head in the direction of the life we really want and the mission we came to accomplish.

KATE'S STORY

Kate was on the path of the creative number 3 with Capricorn wrapped around it. As a twenty-six-year-old health journalist, she enjoyed playing with words and communicating ideas to others. But she was exhausted from deadline pressures and felt that her life had become drudgery.

When a 3-path person gets buried in drudgery, they feel oppressed and miserable and will often develop health issues to make them reinvent. Kate was having symptoms of chronic fatigue accompanied by weekly migraines. It was time to change directions.

While friends and family encouraged her to stay at her "good job," she secretly came to see me. As I explained her need for creativity, inspiration, and fun in her work, as well as a need to work with very real hands-on objects and not just ideas, she wept. "I have always had a dream of opening a vintage-clothing store," she told me. "It makes me happy to think of doing that. I want to dress people in fun, colorful clothes and help them enjoy how they look. I've always loved fashion. But I went to journalism school. How can I waste that?" she asked me.

Kate had come from a very academically focused family (her father was a university professor). She had always made good grades in school, but from the time she was young, going to thrift shops and creating unique outfits for herself and friends was her favorite hobby. "I used to tell my mom about my dream of having my own used-clothing store. But my parents wanted me to have a good education and become a professional. I've put years into my journalism career."

"It's not a waste," I explained. "You'll take that knowledge with you *into your next career. You may not see how right now, but everything is on purpose. You'll eventually see how one career leads into the other."*

Kate made a list of baby steps for opening a vintage-clothing store where her unique gifts and abilities could be used every day. She wrote a business plan, looked for investment partners, and visited other successful vintage stores. The more she looked into it, the more she was sure that bringing her innate creativity and style to the world through fashion was in alignment with her authentic mission and her lifelong passion for vintage clothes. A year later her store opened.

Today Kate is enjoying running a retail business and has developed a loyal customer following who love the innovative ways she puts clothes together. Her health problems have diminished greatly. She recently e-mailed me that she sent a fashion column proposal called "Going Vintage" to a local women's magazine, and they're interested in publishing her column. Now her journalism background is feeding into her career as a vintage-clothing store owner and fashion writer. One career feeds into the next. Today Kate is happier, healthier, on path, and glad that nothing from her past was a wasted effort.

TO SUMMARIZE THIS CHAPTER

♦ Play the five-million-dollar game. You suddenly have five million dollars in your bank account, perfect health, and perfect relationships. Picture what your life would look like.

♦ What career choices will you make when you aren't limited by money? Will you start a business, create a nonprofit foundation, go back to school, write a book? Which of these dreams is most in alignment with your birth-path mission?

◆ When you imagine this career, do you hear a voice inside your head saying, You'll never be able to do that because of . . . ? This is a negative belief trying to keep you from succeeding. Instead of focusing on why you can't manifest what you want, spend some time seeing that amazing life and career as if they were your reality.

◆ First ask yourself, What do I really want? Then see it happening. Those two steps are enough to change your life dramatically.

19

MEDITATIONS ON
YOUR MISSION

I'M RECOMMENDING MEDITATION TO help you tap into your inner GPS system because it's a time-tested and scientifically researched way of quieting your thoughts. You are not your thoughts. Only when you've quieted the constant chatter in your mind can you access your intuition, inner guidance, and know which path and which next step are right for you.

Over the years I've studied every different type of meditation technique from Buddhist to Hindu, Catholic, Christian, kabbalah-based, and New Age. Here's what I've learned.

The techniques taught by the ancient traditions of Hinduism and Buddhism have been tested in scientific labs and reported in scientific journals to be effective ways of quieting and focusing the mind and shifting into alpha brain waves.

To read more about how this works, you can explore books such as *The Relaxation Response,* by Herbert Benson, M.D., which was first published in 1975. Dr. Benson's studies at Boston's Beth Israel Hospital and Harvard Medical School showed that daily practice of techniques such as transcendental meditation can lower blood pressure, reduce heart disease, and enhance clarity of mind and well-being.

Other studies on the benefits of meditation have been reported in journals such as the *Journal of the American Medical Association* (*JAMA*) and the *New England Journal of Medicine* (*NEJM*). Meditation studies are also cited in Joseph Dispenza's fascinating book, *Evolve Your Brain*.

Best-selling author Deepak Chopra, M.D., has an instructional meditation CD called *The Soul of Healing Meditations*, which takes you through a step-by-step process of quieting your thoughts.

Here's a technique I recommend:

1. Use a sound—a word, mantra, prayer, or chant—to quiet your mind. The ancient techniques of following the breath or focusing on the gap between thoughts are too difficult for many Westerners to master and practice on a daily basis. We need to give our monkey minds something to play with so that the thoughts go away and leave us alone. When we repeat a sound, word, prayer, or chant over and over again, it creates a peaceful rhythm in our minds and begins to lure the monkey mind away—leaving us in peace and able to connect with our higher selves and eventually tap into higher realms. I recommend the phrase *Om namah Shivaya*, which means, "I bow to the divine self."

2. Repeat that sound silently in your mind for at least twenty minutes while sitting still and not allowing your head to rest on anything (or you'll fall asleep).

3. When you notice your mind thinking about things, don't get frustrated. Just gently bring the mind back to the sound or word you're repeating.

4. If you do this every day for at least two weeks, you'll begin to notice a shift in your consciousness when you're

meditating—you'll reach a higher vibrational state. You'll eventually get addicted to this higher state and want to meditate every day.

5. At the end of your sitting meditation, you'll notice a gap of quiet, clearheaded space. Voice your request for guidance now. Say, for example, Show me the next step for bringing my destined work to the world. Or pray for your loved ones (wrap them in white light). Or visualize the events you want to have happen in your future, such as the new career or a happy relationship.

6. When you've done that successfully, slowly get up and go back to your routine.

Here are some other kinds of mediations and visualizations you can use to overcome challenges. I teach the first meditation in my workshops, and it has helped many people make peace with a difficult relationship.

BELITTLER MEDITATION

All of us have grown up with someone doubting our abilities. It's the law of human evolution that someone will doubt us. This person plays an important role in our mission; they provide us with something to push against in order to find our way. However, we sometimes get stopped by this person's limited view instead of using our energy to move past it.

These people may say, "Who do you think you are? Be happy for what you have. Why can't you be like everybody else? Just get a job, any job." These statements imply that we have no unique talents or gifts, and therefore should be able to fit successfully into any job we can find.

Recognize that your soul chose to have this person in your life for a reason. The negative message this person is sending you is a negative belief you've carried with you for many lifetimes. You long to eradicate it. Only by having it forced upon you from outside yourself will you find the strength (sometimes through anger) to break the pattern.

These negative people are actually doing an important job by helping you find your power. Be grateful for them.

1. Imagine one of the proudest moments of your life. This could be recent or an event from your childhood. It could be graduating from high school, getting good grades, performing in a play, getting a promotion, writing a book, and so on.

2. Remember that moment and all the praise you received. During that time did anyone in your life say something that deeply hurt your feelings? If so, I'm sure you remember it. Think of it now, and remember who said it to you. Picture that person.

3. Look that person in the eyes and say with love and graciousness, "You may not speak to me that way again. I'm sending you to your room right now."

4. Visualize that person slinking off to their room feeling humbled and acting hurt and sad.

5. When you think of this person from now on, they are no longer powerful in your mind. You are no longer intimidated by them. The words they say no longer have an impact on you.

6. Picture that person crying in their room. From your place of highest wisdom and compassion, go and soothe them. Hold them in your arms comfortingly. You are now their protector and nurturer. You realize how they need love, and how hurt they've been in their life. Feel compassion for them and their life story.

7. Slowly come out of your visualization. From now on when you think of that person, you are comforting, nurturing, and soothing them. They are like a child in need of your love. This is the only way you will think of them.

8. Say to them: "I'm very grateful that you're playing your role in my life drama exactly as I designed it. You're truly helping me learn what I came here to learn. Thank you!"

GETTING IN TOUCH WITH YOUR PASSION

1. Imagine a ray of brilliant yellow light emanating from the area around the center of your chest. Picture it as flaming sunlight pouring out of your chest and shining brightly on everything around you.

2. Hold your hands out, palms facing upward, in front of your chest. Feel the warmth of that light on your hands.

3. Imagine that light spreading out to reach all of your house, your family, your street, and your neighbors. See them basking in it. See them feeling loved and nurtured by this light coming from your heart. See them being healed by it.

4. Spread that light out farther, as far as you can imagine. Comfort someone far away with this warm loving light. Feel the greatness of your heart. Feel the power of your love.

5. Feel that you are nurturing, healing, and comforting all the suffering beings in the world. See them being soothed and loved by the great vast ocean of love within you.

6. Slowly come back to your body. Feel the power of that vast ocean of love that emanated from your chest. Recognize it. Think: My heart is enormous and guides me to the work I came here to do.

A DAY IN THE LIFE

Select a career that you have often considered pursuing. Go through the following exercise in order to get a clear answer about whether or not you should pursue it now:

1. Imagine you have this new career (the one you've often considered pursuing). Picture yourself waking up in the morning, getting dressed, and going to work. Picture your desk or workspace.
2. Notice how your body feels while you visualize this day. How does your throat feel? Restricted or relaxed? How does your stomach feel? How does your chest feel? Are you smiling?
3. Visualize the people you work with—how old they are, how they interact with you, and what your relationships are like. Picture yourself doing the tasks required in this job all day long.
4. Picture yourself coming home from work. You greet your family or friends as you return home. What do you tell them about your day? How do you feel? Check in with your body.
5. Do you feel renewed, excited, refreshed? Is there tension in your body as you imagine this new career? Do you feel excited and happy or depressed and drained when you think of spending a day doing this work? How do you describe this workday to your friends?
6. Did you get a strong yes or no from your body/intuition about this career?

SENDING SAD SADIE OR TERRIBLE TOM ON VACATION

1. Give a name to the part of you that enjoys wallowing in negativity—whether it's Sad Sadie, Mad Matilda, Pitiful Paul, or Terrible Tom. Name the character that lives at the low end of your energy continuum (the "pitiful self").

2. Invite Sadie or Tom to tea. Imagine him or her sitting across the table staring back at you. Have a talk. Be nice.

3. Tell your pitiful self that you appreciate the powerful negative emotion he or she brings to your life because this emotion has inspired you to move forward, whether it's been anger that has fueled you or fear that you've fought to overcome. It has served its purpose in your life.

4. Ask your pitiful self to take a vacation for a while, so that you can get some work done, have a little fun, and relax. Promise your pitiful self you'll invite him or her back again soon because you recognize the value of that negative emotion as a powerful force in your life. Be sweet.

5. See your pitiful self getting up from the table and packing for a trip. Help your pitiful self pack. Wave good-bye at the door, and wrap your pitiful self in white light as he or she walks away.

TO SUMMARIZE THIS CHAPTER

◆ The ancient meditation techniques used in the traditions of Hinduism and Buddhism have been tested in scientific labs and reported in scientific journals to be effective ways of quieting and focusing the mind.

◆ Use a sound—such as a word, mantra, prayer, or chant—to quiet your mind. Sit for at least twenty minutes once or twice a day repeating this sound.

◆ At the end of your sitting meditation, you'll notice a gap of quiet, clearheaded space. Voice your request for higher guidance now.

◆ There are other kinds of meditations and visualizations you can use to overcome challenges—from feeling compassion for someone who may belittle you to sending away the part of yourself that tells you it doubts your competence to opening your heart to find passionate work.

20

TAKING INSPIRED ACTION

AFTER DOING THE INNER explorations described in this book and discovering your birth path and its flavor, it's essential to take action. Go out into the world and research your new ideas. Meet people, network, make phone calls, hand out your résumé and business cards, write a business plan—take tangible action steps in a new direction.

Why? It's a law of physics—once an object begins moving forward it takes on a force (energy) of its own. Once *you* move forward in any direction—even the wrong one—you'll be pulled into the flow of forward-moving energy; you'll be guided to the right people and opportunities. You'll become part of a vortex of positive energy that moves you into the right place at the right time. Forward action takes on a life of its own.

There's another component to taking action. When you make phone calls to research a new direction, meet with someone to discuss an idea, or do research on the Internet, you're sending a message to the universe that you're moving forward. Even if you're not research-ing the exact right direction, your energy will attract opportunities now. Opportunities that will pull you toward your destined work. Our higher guides aren't allow to interfere with us, but once we start moving forward they can open doors.

Inaction, sitting at home worrying or being unhappy, will not open any doors. You *must* take a step forward in a new direction—then doors will open. During my sessions and classes, clients make lists of action steps to take. I ask them to make a commitment to follow up on those items, even if they're not sure about the direction.

When we meet again they report what happened when they made that phone call, researched the school, or met with someone on their list. These simple acts always produce results, whether it's a gut feeling that this is the right direction for them to pursue now or not. Either way these actions lead to another meeting or another phone call. My clients look better, sound better, and *feel* better than they did when they were stagnating—not taking action.

"But I'm still not sure which direction to go in," you may say. That doesn't matter a hoot, I say. (You actually *do* know.)

Choose three possible career directions that interest you after determining that they line up with your birth path. Investigate one career by meeting or calling people, doing Internet searches, and so on. If nothing opens up after two weeks, investigate your second choice for two weeks. It's that simple. You're going to follow the good energy, wherever it takes you.

The results of your action steps depend on your energy! In other words, the more positive high-end energy—happiness, optimism, divinity, and inspiration—you can pump through your body before making any phone calls or going to any meetings, the better the outcomes will be.

Pump your energy by dreaming of the life you want, imagining you already have it, asking for divine guidance, exercising, meditating, and sending out positive energy to everyone you interact with.

Before making any phone calls, stand up, walk around, laugh out loud, and smile while you make the call. Before going to any meetings put on an outfit that makes you happy, go for a thirty-minute daydreaming walk, and call someone who makes you laugh.

Always script meetings first by seeing them happening the way you want them to. Visualize all meetings and phone calls ending with good feelings all around and new possibilities being discussed. Feel the good energy you'll be feeling when you walk out of the meeting. See smiles and warm handshakes all around.

Endlessly complaining about your unhappiness won't help you; neither will watching television, worrying, being angry or afraid, giving up, getting drunk, or taking drugs. Being unhappy is not an option. Learn about your birth path and the flavor of your work, pump your energy to the high end of your continuum, dream of what you want, laugh, see a coach or counselor who makes you move forward, ask for divine guidance, meditate, take three action steps in *any* new career direction.

I'll say it again: Take a step in any possible career direction. Pump the good energy until you're in the flow. You'll get pulled in the right direction.

SEARCH WITH INTUITION

While you're out researching new career possibilities, practice using your intuition to guide you. For example, before making an important phone call meditate for a few minutes, seeing the person you're about to call.

Connect with them on an intuitive level until you have pictures in your mind of what they look like. Do they feel happy, sad, joyful, or negative? Get a feeling for the emotional state they're in.

When you can feel how they're feeling, decide if calling them today is going to be in your highest good or not. If they feel negative, you have a choice. You can meditate on the person, wrapping them in white light and gratitude until they feel better, and then call them. Or you can wait until another time when they feel more positive to you intuitively before you call.

Before going to a job interview meditate on what the office looks like and how the energy feels. See it in your mind's eye. Then meditate on sending gratitude and white light into that office before your interview. This paves the way for your visit by raising the vibrations of the office. It also gives you a precursor of important information about the kind of energy that dominates that workplace and whether you would feel comfortable there every day or not.

Eventually it will become second nature to visit places through your intuition before you ever really step into them. This will give you quite an advantage when job hunting or networking for a new business.

Now your higher self as well as your posse of divine guides are guiding you. This is a much more powerful approach then letting ego and will drive you forward—which feels more like a bull in a china shop. Following your intuition puts you in the flow of the forces of life. It allows you to work for your and everyone else's highest good. It allows the force to be with you.

SAMANTHA'S STORY

Samantha's high-powered New York lifestyle looked great from the outside. At twenty-nine, she had accomplished everything she'd set her mind on when she launched out of school with a degree in finance.

She was well paid, well respected, and working in the investment banking field in real estate acquisitions.

But life didn't feel good on the inside. Her important love relationship had recently crumbled, and the thrill had long gone out of her daily work routine. She was depressed enough that her doctor prescribed antidepressants—a sure sign of being off path.

When I meditated on her mission, it was clear she was in the midst of a major wake-up call—the first Saturn returning that hits between ages twenty-seven and thirty. This is the time when we realize that we've lived up to the external expectations of family and culture, and yet we're unfulfilled. And she was in a 5 personal year, which meant it was time for change and expansion.

Samantha was on the path of the number 3 with Pisces wrapped around it. This gave her a creative and brilliant mind combined with intense intuition. Of course she would be successful in finance. But was it the work she came here to do? Her own answer to that question was an emphatic no.

I explained to Samantha that she was a born teacher and writer, here to show others how to connect to their own intuition and creativity. Hearing these words, she began to cry. "I took a trip to South America last year and met a shaman there. He told me the same thing. I wanted to stay and study shamanism with him. But I didn't. It wasn't realistic or practical to think I could make my living doing that."

But she still longed for that ancient, intuitive knowledge. Since her meeting with the shaman, she had filled dozens of journals with ideas and insights into the need for intuition and creativity in the workplace. Even though she had a natural ability to bring those traits to work with her, she recognized that many others didn't. The action steps we listed included studying shamanism where she lived, writing the outline for a class based on bringing intuition to the workplace, and building a Web site.

Over the next few months, Samantha found a local class on shamanism that she could attend on weekends. By disciplining herself to work at *the computer every Sunday morning, she created content that became the foundation for her consulting business based on teaching creativity and intuition to executives. She used her shamanic training to bring depth and authenticity to her content. Her journals became the foundation for future books and workshops.*

While still working at her investment banking job, she built a Web site that launched her business as a corporate consultant teaching executives to use their power creatively and intuitively in the workplace. As the next step she offered to teach a workshop called "Using Intuition in the Workplace" for the company she worked for, and they loved it. A friend who worked for another company invited her to teach a workshop for their employees, and she did.

Samantha was afraid at first of taking the leap and letting go of her old, secure job. Slowly, by taking little action steps, she accumulated clients and confidence for this new direction.

She recently wrote, "It's almost magical the way my old skills from finance have fed into my new career as an intuition-into-business consultant and teacher. I see a future that's rich with teaching, writing, and shamanic studies. I may even become a modern-day shaman someday—a New York version of one."

A FINAL NOTE: WHEN ALL ELSE FALLS AWAY

When all else is stripped away there's a great beauty inside you. It's your authentic self—the one who came here on a mission. This *will* be the year you remember your impossible mission and realign your life to accomplish it.

The purpose of your confusion is growth and change. Once you change directions confusion ceases and clarity slips in. The purpose of your pain is to strip away the trappings of who you're not—to leave you bare and raw, naked like a newborn and clear about what you've come to do.

Have you had your heart broken by a lover? Felt betrayed by your own children? Watched your health fall apart? Been disappointed by a career that didn't make you happy and wealthy? Of course you have. It ripped your soul jagged on purpose.

Feel the pain in your heart, embrace it, weep it out, shed it through your pores until your spirit is cleansed and shiny. Look into the mirror at your face now—open and surrendered, innocent and sweet.

That *is* who you are, by the way—a naked sweet soul who landed here on a difficult journey and got just a little lost. Try to remember who you were before the trappings and titles, the successes and failures, the burdens and expectations.

Embrace that naked soul, that wide-open innocent face, and ask yourself, What's the gift I came to share?

Ignore anyone who tells you that sharing your gift won't make money. Embrace your higher knowledge and say aloud, "When I'm living true to what I came to do and working from my gifts, I attract abundance and success because I'm in alignment with divine order."

"I'm in alignment with divine order. . . ."

Kiss those words as they slip past your tongue in whispers because you're hardly able to speak them, much less believe them. Open your mouth wide and shout until the room echoes those words back to you.

Clean your house, throw out the furniture, open the windows, sweat out your past indulgences, and pray for a blessing of fresh air. Embrace the prickly tingle of dawn breaking through the shimmering snow of an icy winter. Take a timid step in a scary new direction that has beckoned you for lifetimes. It will feel like spring.

Who do you think you are to ignore the potential you set out to accomplish in this lifetime? Who do you think you are to believe that your pain is greater than everyone else's? Don't you understand the hidden sorrow behind every perfect household, every career success, every accolade or boastful moment from siblings and friends?

We are all on this overwhelming journey together, trying to evolve as a species, to reach the great unknown human potential. This requires effort.

You signed up for this tour of duty. Don't go AWOL now. There still may be a child you can save from the streets or a mother who needs your blessings. But you'll never know until you follow your true work, accomplish your preprogrammed mission, quit playing it small and trying to be like anyone else.

Listen to your loud voice in the empty room shouting, "I'm in alignment with divine order when I'm doing the work I came to do!"

Wake up from the slumber of your exhausting journey. Yes, you've had some setbacks. But you wanted to. You knew how far off course you were. Pinch yourself. Take a big breath. Say, "I am a divine energy being, not a bumbling human in a body suit doomed to a pitiful existence. And now I *will* live as if I know that."

You brought powerful gifts with you from the highest realms in order to use them to make the world a better place through your work. And you've known what these gifts were and what your mission was since you were very young, but you've been talked out of believing in it.

Getting your life lined up with your mission and gifts isn't as hard as you think. Remember what and whom you've lost already—sacrificed on the trail of your higher education. Your intuition is constantly trying to push you in a brave new direction; it's probably why you picked up this book.

Ask yourself these questions:

When all else falls away, who am I inside? When I look back at the trail of my tarnished trophies and sad memories, what secret lesson do I see?

This is your first step forward into new territory. Like a toddler unsteady on his or her feet, you will find your new beginning on this auspicious journey. You always knew it would be worth the great effort of a lifetime. And you, of all people, don't believe in wasted time. This is your year to just do it.

When everything is stripped away, who's left? That's the point of your painful story, isn't it? In those moments of deep soul-searching surrender—walking alone on a beach contemplating life—what part of you do you find again? That stripped-bare part of yourself is your holy grail, your pot of gold, the reason you came here, and the name of your gift.

Who do you remember being when you were young and free? Where did that person go?

When you turn off the TV, unplug the iPod, put down the paper, and get quiet, who do you find in your head? Your higher self is still in there, you know, eager to help you find your way.

Stop defending, blaming, excusing, chatting, and doing—just for a little while, and turn your focus slightly inward. You'll hear that powerful navigation code pulsing in your heart. It's whispering, Try this career, call that person, quit that job, take this class.

Imagine if you did just one of those things today. . . .

TO SUMMARIZE THIS CHAPTER

- ◆ After discovering your birth path and its flavor, it's essential to take action. Go out into the world and research new ideas that are in alignment with your path.

- ◆ Once *you* move forward in any direction—even the wrong one—you'll be pulled into the flow of forward-moving energy; you'll be guided to the right people and opportunities.

- While you're out researching new career possibilities, practice using your intuition to guide you. This will give you an advantage because you'll feel when it's right to contact someone.

- Use your high-end positive energy to attract opportunities. Pump positive energy into every phone call and interview, and you'll get positive results

PART
5

THE WAKE-UP
WORKBOOK

21

SIX STEPS TO REMEMBERING WHAT YOU CAME HERE TO DO

1. Tap into Your Intuitive Career Guidance System
2. Own Your Power
3. Find Your Destiny Path
4. Let Talents and Dreams Guide You
5. Use Your Pain as Fuel
6. Put It All Together and Go!

ARE YOU DOING THE WORK you came here to do? Living the life you came here to live? These six steps will guide you to the work you've already signed up for.

In this workbook you'll explore new career possibilities, own up to who you truly are, read your unique destiny path, gain insight into your changing career cycles, and create a practical plan for moving forward.

Here are six ways to find the work you came here to do.

STEP 1

TAP INTO YOUR INTUITIVE
CAREER GUIDANCE SYSTEM

To find your destined work path it's essential to tap into your own intuitive guidance. Without understanding that each answer you need is already available to you, you're at the mercy of every passing opinion or criticism of your life, which will certainly throw you off course.

The first step is realizing that you are not your thoughts. You are an energy being—a pulsing wave of light connected to the energetic fabric of which the entire universe is made. In quantum physics this is known as the membrane theory, which says we are all made of the same stuff—pulsing waves of light that connect everything and everyone in the universe.

You are not your physical body or the crazy thoughts that your mind creates. Your higher self knows this and doesn't identify with the limitations of the "seen" world. Your higher self is the only place you should go for guidance.

You can tap into your higher self through prayer and meditation and by using your intuition. Getting this kind of information is a very different process from using your mind to guide you, which can take you far from the destiny you've come here to fulfill. The correct course of action requires sitting still and shutting up—at least once a day.

Learn to stop the constant chatter of your mind that fills your head with fear and negative beliefs about what's possible for you. There's a science to creating alpha brain waves—the quiet place where chatter ceases.

Many spiritual traditions have this formula figured out. Whether you choose to repeat a prayer such as the Our Father, a mantra (sa-cred word or phrase such as *Om namah Shivaya*), or to follow your breath, you will begin to experience the consciousness inside you that is separate from and greater than your mind. This will help you understand that you are a great, wise, and powerful energetic being connected to the divine fabric that intertwines us with all other ener-getic beings in the universe.

EXERCISE

1 Sit comfortably without letting your head lean against anything (a sure way to fall asleep). Take several deep re-leasing breaths.

2 Silently repeat either *Om namah Shivaya* or the Our Father or another sound of your choice. Sit for ten min-utes silently repeating these words. When you notice your mind wandering to other thoughts, gently bring it back to your mantra or prayer. Don't struggle. Be gentle.

3 After ten minutes, slowly stop repeating the words. In this quiet gap before getting up and going back to your routine, ask for guidance. Say, "Show me my next step for manifesting my destined work."

RAISE YOUR VIBRATIONS

When we're emitting a low vibration (because of fatigue, negative thoughts, or negative feelings), we're not capable of connecting with our higher guidance.

How do we raise our energy? Prayer, chanting, meditation

(especially the Lord's Prayer), openhearted laughter, gratitude, and sweetness all increase our frequency level. We can also raise our energy by shifting the focus of our thoughts away from what's troubling us to what we would prefer. This simple shift of focus helps immediately.

Inspiring music, art, and physical endeavors can also shift us to a higher frequency. Dreaming of what we want to happen (especially when it makes us giggle) is another great way to speed up frequency. No matter how desperate you feel, shift out of your fear and negativity when you ask for help. It's the only way to access higher guidance. After awhile, you'll recognize the difference between high- or low-level guidance. Never listen to guidance that makes you feel uncomfortable or afraid.

EPR = GOOD VIBRATIONS

My favorite technique for quickly raising energy to a higher vibration is what I call EPR—energetic personal resuscitation. These three quick emergency switches for changing your energy are humor, gratitude, and sweetness.

Use these energy-saving techniques quickly and effectively in any emergency situation where your energy is at the lower end of your continuum. By switching to any of these feelings, you'll rise higher on your continuum and thus be better able to respond to the challenge.

Humor is a very quick and easy way to tap into source energy. When we laugh with big, openhearted, unrestrained laughter, we're recognizing the absurdity of life. We start to see the big picture. We start connecting to our higher guidance.

Gratitude is a high-vibration feeling. When you get it pulsing through you, you'll feel opened up and receptive to source energy. Gratitude works especially well to counteract anger. By sending this high-level emotion to someone you have conflict with, the conflict will begin to soften. You will no longer be a victim to this relationship.

Sweetness means showing our true sweet selves to others, which allows them to open up and show us their sweetness. It's like holding a baby. We see the sweetness and go there to join it. If we switch to sweetness in the midst of conflict, we'll see instant positive results and a better resolution. Try it!

EXERCISE

1 Write an example of a challenging situation—and your response—where you used one of these quick switches to make it turn out better than it started.

2 Describe a current situation in your life and how you will improve it with humor, sweetness, or gratitude.

STATE YOUR REQUEST

Since the human experience includes freedom of choice, our guides aren't allowed to interfere in our lives. They can't step in without an invitation; they wait until we make a request, and then they're required to help. (It's their job.)

At the end of your daily meditation or throughout the day, say or write: "Show me the path I came in to manifest for my highest good. I'm ready to move forward."

Whenever you doubt you'll find your true work, say: "I am already being guided to use my gifts and talents to make the world a better place in my unique way." When contemplating a new career, examine if this new work is in alignment with this statement. If so, go after it.

PRACTICE EVERY DAY

Get into the practice of pausing and tapping into your intuition before making an important phone call, going to a meeting, or making a big decision. When you start listening to your higher self, things will go more smoothly in your life. You didn't sign up for this lifetime to go it alone. You knew you had a posse of higher beings who would guide you along the way. It's time to remember that and make good use of that guidance, so you can fulfill the destiny you came here to achieve.

EXERCISE

Think of someone you're planning to call today. Close your eyes, calm your mind, and ask, "Should I call that person today? Are they in a good space? How will the conversation go if I call today?" Wait until you get an answer (such as a feeling, a voice, or a vision) that feels as if it comes from some place other than your chatty mind. (Other examples of situations in which this exercise might apply include: "Should I take this route home or another route?" "Should I talk to my manager about that problem today or tomorrow?" "What does this person I'm about to meet look and feel like?" "Where is my child/spouse/sibling right now, and what are they doing?")

STEP 2

OWN YOUR POWER

All of us have a million reasons to feel bad at any given moment of our day. Circumstances change for the better and for the worse in a constant flow of events. We react to those circumstances as our families, teachers, and friends have taught us to. We believe we have little choice in how we react. And even if we did react in a different way, what would it matter? This is truly the "human condition."

Scientists and spiritual teachers alike have aligned themselves behind one idea—everything is energy. Everything you see, sit on, feel—the sun on your face, children's laughter, a good run, prayer, a great kiss—is all source energy: the divine vibration everything and everyone came from.

You're composed of this same energy, and its frequency can be raised or lowered according to your thoughts, feelings, and beliefs. The frequency you send out at any given time attracts like frequencies. Like attracts like.

For example, when you're feeling joy and gratitude, your vibration puts you on a plane where you can connect with and attract other elements that vibrate on the higher plane. Thus you can bring wonderful things into your life when you're feeling good. (Haven't you noticed this is true? When you're having a great day, more wonderful things happen to you all day long. When you're having a bad day, things seem to get worse and worse, don't they?)

Here's the surprise: These ups and downs are because of *your* energy, not because of external forces working on you. Each of us has an energy continuum—negative at the bottom, positive at the top. Positive energy includes our brilliance, goodness, divinity, inspiration, love, passion, optimism, happiness, and joy (our connectedness).

Negative energy includes our anger, depression, sadness, guilt, pessimism, meanness, sense of lack, drudgery, and separateness—not only from others, but from our source energy.

Everyday we bounce up and down on this continuum, reacting to our circumstances. We say, If only my circumstances would change I could be happy. The ultimate irony is that if we get happy, our circumstances will change to meet us.

Moving up your energy continuum (in spite of circumstances) by changing your energy to a higher frequency and opening up to source energy connects you to inspiration, spirituality, and goodness. It changes your life for the better.

You can imagine your energy continuum as a fuel gauge. When the fuel tank in your car nears empty, you worry about running out of gas and being stranded—which is separateness and stagnation. When it's full, you're confident and able to explore. You have unlimited energy and ideas—which is connectedness, inspiration, and productivity.

You're in control of what level you vibrate on, thus you're in control of what happens to you on any given day. Your emotions determine what level you're vibrating on. When you feel love and joy, you're at the highest level attracting the most wonderful things into your life. When you're feeling despair, you attract more of the same.

No matter how positive your energy is, you will still have challenging events, or karmas, happen to you. We sign up for these karmas in order to evolve. However, your reaction to these difficult events determines their outcome. Your energy level determines whether you react well or poorly to a crisis. A good life requires good energy. It's that simple. So what fills your energy tank?

EXERCISE

Draw a graph of your continuum from high to low. Write words next to the top, middle, and bottom that describe your personal emotional traits at each point. For example, next to the top you could write "funny," "excited," or "talking frequently." At the bottom you could write "sullen," "quiet," "not laughing," "weepy," or whatever your personal behaviors are at each point.

    ———————

    ———————

    ———————

    ———————

    ———————

    ———————

NAME YOUR CHARACTERS

Name the part of you that lives at the bottom end of your energy continuum—whether it's Sad Sadie, Terrible Tom, or Worthless Wanda. This is who we playfully call the "pitiful self." Give it a name so that you know who is showing up in your life. You don't want to leave your big decisions—such as "How am I going to make a living?"—to your pitiful self. Describe your pitiful self and what it thinks you should do for a living.

Now name your brilliant self—the part of you who lives at the high-end of your continuum and is brilliant, powerful, optimistic, smart, and inspired. This could be Awesome Aretha, Powerful Paula, or Magnificent Michael. Describe your brilliant self and what it thinks you should do for a living.

What have you learned from this exercise?

SOLUTIONS VS. PROBLEMS: THE PROPER FOCUS

How do you feel when you think about your problems? Do you toss and turn at night worrying about your job, money, relationships, or health?

Do you sense how this low-end negativity brings you down? When we focus on the problems, our energy sinks to the low end of our continuum. And our problems get bigger. (What we focus on always gets bigger, because our thoughts give it energy.)

One of the fastest ways to feel happier and have more energy in your day is to focus on at least three potential solutions to every problem that worries you. This shifts the mind from limited, negative thinking to open, creative, source-energy thinking that welcomes new possibilities. No more focusing and fretting on your insurmountable problems.

EXERCISE

Write three problems facing you right now and below each one write a positive solution.

Problems:
(I can't find work that I love that creates abundance for me.)

1.

2.

3.

Solutions:

(I'm using my positive energy while taking action steps to attract work in alignment with my mission—which will create abundance for me.)

1.

2.

3.

NEGATIVE BELIEFS AND THEIR SOLUTIONS

It's important to realize how your negative beliefs are creating your reality. When you think, Well, it doesn't matter how hard I work, I never get recognition, the universal source feels that low-end-vibration belief and provides you abundantly with more of the same negative energy to match what you're sending out. The source energy aligns itself with your belief and says, Make it so!

The first step is recognizing your negative beliefs.

EXERCISE

Write three negative beliefs that are haunting you today and write positive antidotes to them.

EXAMPLE: No matter how hard I work I never make enough money.

ANTIDOTE: When I work from the high end of my energy continuum, and my work is in alignment with my birth path, financial abundance flows gracefully into my life.

EXAMPLE: The economy is so bad that there aren't any good jobs.

ANTIDOTE: When I use my positive energy to look for a job that's in alignment with my mission, I attract wonderful opportunities that I can't even begin to imagine now.

Negative beliefs about life:

    1.

    2.

    3.

Antidotes:

    1.

    2.

    3.

THE ENERGY OF MONEY

Consider the possibility that money is energy too. And consider the possibility that one of the things stopping you from having financial ease and abundance is your negative thinking about money. Can you imagine yourself wealthy and living a life of ease? Can you picture it? Many people can't. Write three negative beliefs you have about money. Write their antidotes below them.

Negative beliefs about money:
(I'll never make enough money to . . .)

    1.

    2.

    3.

Positive antidotes:

(When my work is in alignment with my path, I will attract . . .)

1.

2.

3.

STEP 3

FIND YOUR DESTINY PATH

When you chose to drop into this dense realm, you outlined a plan for your journey—a road map with certain destinations highlighted for your visit.

You wanted to take part in the great human adventure.

You signed up.

You said, "Okay, I'll experience some grief and loss to help me learn greater compassion, and I'll need constant reminders along the way of who I am and what I'm here to do. If I get really lost, I'll design a powerful challenge to kick me back on path."

This detailed life mission was encoded into your name and the date of your birth—which can be reduced to a simple numerological code first identified by Pythagoras.

In his system every number from 1 through 9 has a positive and negative vibration (which shows its potential and challenges). Your destiny number—derived from your birth date—is a picture of the mission you came here to achieve, along with the potential pitfalls of your path. By understanding this you can make wise choices for your career.

In numerology all numbers are reduced to the digits 1 through 9 except for two cosmic vibrations symbolized by the master numbers 11 and 22.

All other numbers are reduced to the basic digits 1 through 9 by adding the digits of the entire number together.

For example, the number 43 equals 7 (4 + 3 = 7), and 10 equals 1 (1 + 0 = 1).

Every letter of the alphabet also corresponds to the numbers 1 through 9. For example, A = 1, B = 2, C = 3, and so on.

In your calculations, reduce all numbers down to a single digit, except for the master numbers 11 and 22, which stay as 11/2 and 22/4.

Calculate your birth path here:

Your birth month:
Your birth date:
Your birth year:

Total:

....

Reduced down to a single digit:

Your birth-path or destined-work number:

(See chapter 7 for a full description of your birth-path number.)

EXERCISE

After learning about your birth-path number and what that means, write your thoughts about how this applies to your life:

What have you learned from this?
Discuss it with your partner.

THE FLAVOR OF YOUR SUN SIGN

You probably already know your astrological sun sign and have been told that it reveals certain traits about you. Or you may have had an astrological reading done and learned a more powerful, in-depth way of looking at your journey. How does numerology interface with astrology? In many ways. We're going to keep it simple here and focus on how your sun sign interacts with and flavors your birth path.

Aries (Ram) = March 21–April 19
Taurus (Bull) = April 20–May 20
Gemini (Twins) = May 21–June 21
Cancer (Crab) = June 22–July 22
Leo (Lion) = July 23–August 22
Virgo (Virgin) = August 23–September 22
Libra (Scales) = September 23–October 23
Scorpio (Scorpion) = October 24–November 21
Sagittarius (Archer) = November 22–December 21
Capricorn (Goat) = December 22–January 19
Aquarius (Water Bearer) = January 20–February 18
Pisces (Fish) = February 19–March 20

Combine your birth-path number with your sun sign here:

Birth path:

Sun sign:

(For a full description of how your sun sign affects your birth path see chapter 9.)

My combination of birth path and sun sign gives me these insights about my mission:

YOUR CURRENT CAREER CYCLE

Every year of your life you've been under the influence of a particular number—1 through 9, 11, or 22. Since all of our learning and evolution takes place within the vibrational range of these numbers, you're working with a different type of energy each year, within a repeating nine-year cycle.

This is all on purpose, of course. It's part of your plan. As you look back at your life, tracing the nine-year cycles, you'll see the repeating patterns of reinvention in your life. You'll realize how you've gotten better at mastering certain challenges and better at letting go of what no longer serves you.

You started this lifetime in the vibration of the path you chose. If your path is the number 5, then the first year of your life was a 5 personal year. The second year of your life was a 6 personal year, and so on.

By adding up your day, month, and year of birth, you'll find your path number as well as the personal year that began your journey. You've repeated those nine-year cycles throughout your life.

Your current personal year is determined by the single-digit numbers of your birth month and birth date added to the current calendar year and reduced to a single digit (or a master number 11 or 22).

For example, someone with a birthday of September 15, 1951—during 2009—would be experiencing an 8 personal year.

Birth month: September = 9
Birth date: 15 equals 6 (1 + 5 = 6)
Current year: 2009 equals 11 = 2 (2 + 0 + 0 + 9 = 11 = 1 + 1 = 2)

Add 9 (birth month) + 6 (birth date) + 2 (current year) to get
personal year = 8 (9 + 6 + 2 = 17 = 1 + 7 = 8)

Even though this person would be experiencing an 8 personal year during the calendar year 2009, by September 2009 they would feel the beginnings of their 9 personal year (which coincides with the calendar year 2010).

Let's compute your personal year here:

Your birth month:
Your birth date:
Current year:

Total:

Reduced to a single digit:

This is your personal year:

(For a full description of personal years and how they influence career, see chapter 10.)

EXERCISE

After discovering the personal year you're in and how those energetic influences are affecting your life, what new insights did you gain about your career?

How might this knowledge influence your choices this year and next year?

MY PATH SUMMARY

I'm on a ___ birth path, which means my destined work is about:

The flavor of my path is influenced by my sun sign, which is:

This sun-sign flavor brings these traits to my mission:

The highest evolution of my birth-path mission is realized by:

I'm off path when I'm living through the lower vibration of my birth path, which feels like:

When this happens, I can improve the course of my life by:

I'm currently in a(n) _____ personal year within my nine-year cycle.

This means that I should focus on:

Next year's energy will bring:

STEP 4

LET TALENTS AND DREAMS GUIDE YOU

Your talents show you what you came here to do. You brought them from the higher realms and from other lifetimes to use them in your work—to make the world a better place. Every talent you bring is on purpose and acts as a powerful guide to finding the work you came here to do.

Your natural talents are the things you love doing every day. They're the unique, natural gifts that flow easily and gracefully through you. Talents are different from your learned skills, such as computer programming or accounting.

To identify your talents, think about those things you find yourself longing to do even on your days off, such as organizing a room, inspiring others to meet a goal, communicating complex information in a way that others can understand, solving problems, creating beautiful things, and so on.

From the list on the following pages, pick your top five talents and write them here:

1.

2.

3.

4.

5.

I have an ability to

- Organize
- Motivate
- Mediate
- Instruct
- Manage
- Execute
- Lead
- Inspire
- Counsel
- Empower
- Make things work (mechanically)
- Build things
- Design things
- Heal
- Put people at ease
- Contemplate
- Philosophize
- Plan
- Arrange things beautifully
- Sing
- Make music with instruments
- Make beautiful things
- Perform
- Entertain
- Communicate through speech
- Tell stories that instruct

- Be playful
- Persist
- Perceive the essential
- Juggle many responsibilities or activities
- Be efficient
- Be loyal
- Be appropriate
- Be self-disciplined
- Be tolerant
- Concentrate
- Love
- Be happy
- Be balanced
- Be generous
- Be compassionate
- Be dignified
- Be tender
- Be strong
- Be impeccable
- Be popular
- Be enthusiastic
- Express through writing
- Express through movement
- Express through visual arts
- Express through music
- Analyze
- Be persuasive
- Synthesize ideas

- Be logical
- Think abstractly
- Imagine
- Visualize
- Be athletic
- Be tactical
- Strategize
- Interpret
- Translate languages
- Make things grow
- Negotiate
- Protect or defend
- Invent things
- Evaluate or judge
- Explore or discover

- Experiment
- Nurture
- Invest
- Cooperate
- Inspect
- Investigate
- Plan
- Discern
- Perceive opportunities
- Clarify
- Harmonize
- Establish rapport
- Be decisive
- Initiate or begin
- Complete or conclude

WHAT DO YOU VALUE MOST?

Whatever feels deeply important to you is on purpose: to guide you to the work you came here to do. What's important to you in your career? Helping others? Being creative? These values provide another important clue in your search for your destined work path. Here are some examples:

- Adventure
- Aesthetics
- Creativity
- Helping others
- Independence
- Power
- Recognition

- Security
- Time freedom
- Change and variety
- Affiliation
- Competition
- Community
- Excitement

- Fast pace
- Friendships
- Influencing people
- Inspiration
- Intellectual status
- Knowledge
- Location
- Making decisions
- Moral fulfillment

- Physical challenge
- Profit and gain
- Public contact
- Stability
- Supervision
- Working alone
- Working under pressure
- Working with others

Write yours:

1.

2.

3.

4.

5.

If you decided to write a book about a subject you were *passionately* interested in, what book would you write? Give it a title:

WHAT DO YOU DREAM ABOUT?

Your dreams are the key to your destined work. Play the five-million-dollar game: Pretend I've just given you five-million dollars. You don't have to tell anyone else about the money. It's all yours. I've also given you perfect health and loving relationships. Any health concerns that you've struggled with are gone. Your body feels energized and completely healthy. Any relationships that have been troubling you are now healed. You have perfect love in your life.

Feel the energy shift inside you as you imagine this new life of limitless options. Take a deep breath and feel it. What vacation would you take first? Describe it:

You've come back from your extended vacation and you're completely rested. Now you must choose a career that you would love. You still have abundant money, loving relationships, and perfect health. What career would you choose? Write it here:

From that place of unlimited possibility, write ten careers you've often dreamed of. Whether they're silly or serious, write them here:

DREAMY CAREERS

1.

2.

3.

4.

5.

6.

7.

8.

9.

10.

Review the list you wrote above. Put your hand over each career and notice what feelings or sensations you get when you picture yourself doing this work. Do you feel happy and inspired or heavy and tired? Make notes about your intuitive reactions to the list of careers. Put stars beside the three careers that intuitively feel best to you.

Now analyze each of the careers on your list to see if it's in alignment with your birth-path mission and the flavor of that work as seen in your sun sign. Ask yourself, If I pick this career, is my everyday work fulfilling my mission as expressed in my birth path?

List the careers that are in alignment with what you came to accomplish:

List the careers that intuitively felt best to you:

Which career ideas fall into both of the categories above?

Write three dreams you will manifest before you die:

1.

2.

3.

The question is *not*: "What work can I do?"
The question *is*: "What work would I love doing?"

STEP 5

USE YOUR PAIN AS FUEL

Consider the possibility that all of your pain—every wound you've ever experienced, from loss to illness to disappointment—was exactly what you needed and chose in order to arrive at this point in your life, which is exactly where you're supposed to be.

And imagine that you've chosen (consciously or unconsciously) every important job you've had because it was healing you. What pain needs healing now? Let that answer guide you to your next career step.

Our work heals us by letting us offer to the world exactly what we need to heal ourselves.

Say this out loud: "I am moving forward and using my pain as fuel to do work that makes the world a better place—in my unique way."

EXERCISE

1. When I was a child, what caused me the greatest pain and why?
2. In my entire life, what caused me the greatest pain and why?
3. What pain is calling my attention right now?
4. When I look at my answers, I gain these insights into my career:

By facing your pain, you turn it into energy. It becomes your ally and moves you forward.

WHAT YOU WILL HAVE IN YOUR NEXT JOB

Make a list of everything you need in a career to be happy. Start each item with, "I will have . . ." For example, "I will have time flexibility."

1.

2.

3.

4.

5.

YOUR INTENTION

I intend to use my unique talents of_____ in a way that's in harmony with my values of_____ and in alignment with my birth-path mission, which is about _____.

IS FEAR STOPPING YOU?

Well . . . *duh!*

Fear of failure is simply *fear*. And fear is at the low end of your energy continuum. It's your negativity. Whenever you operate from fear of failure, things don't turn out well. You actually attract negativity into your life with your fear.

EXERCISE

This is what I'm most afraid of:
This is what I'll do to overcome that fear:

Examples:
I'm most afraid of not making enough money.
To overcome that fear, I'll be sure my work is in alignment
    with my birth-path mission (which is the only way to be
    successful), and I'll use powerful positive energy to
    manifest new opportunities for myself.

To counteract fear, change your energy to the high end, and operate from optimism, happiness, and inspiration. Align yourself with what you came to do, and impossible doors will open to help you become successful.

Maybe you are aware of how your fear of failure is stopping you.

Consider that you may have a fear of success that sabotages you even more. Have you ever thought: Who do I think I am to want great success and wealth?

Do you believe that few people ever get true success or happiness and you're not worthy of being one of them? Have you ever succeeded at something impressive and then questioned if you were worthy of that achievement?

Our biggest fear is usually the fear of how powerful and magnificent we really are. It's terrifying to believe in our greatness. Because then we have to live up to it.

Believing we are capable of creating whatever life we want goes against every message we've ever been taught. If we believe what we've been taught—humans are limited beings with limited capacity for happiness—we settle for a "normal" life and limited amounts of *everything*.

We can blame our failures on everything and everyone but ourselves. Dare yourself to break out of this limited thinking.

Write your negative beliefs about what you deserve:

1. Only selfish (or extremely brilliant) people make lots of money and have easy lives.

2.

3.

Now write the positive affirmations to reverse those beliefs:

1. I will work in alignment with my birth-path mission and from the high end of my continuum, which will attract great wealth and ease that I'll use to help others.

2.

3.

STEP 6

PUT IT ALL TOGETHER AND GO!

After doing the explorations described above, it's essential to take action. Go out into the world and research new ideas. Meet people, network, make phone calls, take tangible action steps in a new direction.

It's a law of physics that once an object begins moving forward it takes on a force (energy) of its own. Once you move forward in any direction—even the wrong direction—you'll be pulled into the flow of forward-moving energy, and you'll be guided to the right people and opportunities.

You'll become part of a vortex of positive energy that moves you into the right place at the right time; forward energy takes on a life of its own.

Here are some examples of taking positive action:

Call two people who are working in the career you're interested in. Ask them how they got started and how they like it. Ask for advice and connections.

Research your new career on the Internet and make three phone calls based on what you've learned.

Write a brochure or business plan for your new business idea.

Get résumé help or create a powerful new résumé yourself.

Write three steps you can take this week to start your new career:

1.

2.

3.

ALWAYS SCRIPT THE FUTURE YOU WANT
BEFORE TAKING ACTION

Consider the possibility that if you spent even a couple minutes each day seeing positive outcomes for all your "worries" your life would go in a better direction. Isn't it worth a little experimenting?

When we dream and imagine what we want to happen, we tap into source energy. We tap into the boundless realm of ever-changing possibilities—rather than our limited view of fixed outcomes, which is all we can see from the bottom end of our continuum.

By changing our negative beliefs about what is possible and seeing instead positive outcomes to our challenges, we set the energy in place to make what we want happen. This is called scripting.

Before going to the job interview that you "know you won't get," or before asking a banker for a new business loan, take a moment and see the interaction going beautifully with everyone operating from their high end (especially you).

See the banker saying, "Yes, I think we can put something together to help you launch your business." See the company CEO saying, "We're always looking for people like you. When can you start?" See lots of laughter and good feeling in the room. Feel how happy you'll be after the meeting.

First ask, "What do I really want?" Then see it happening. Those two steps are enough to change your life dramatically.

EXERCISE

Write what you want to happen in your next job interview (or when getting your first new client):

Where do I want my life to be in six months?

What do I want my life to look like in one year?

Now let's go for the big dream! Write down what you want your perfect life to look like in five years:

Where will you be living?

What will your career be?

How much money will be in your bank account?

LET'S SUMMARIZE

While doing the previous steps you've identified your predestined birth path, the flavor your sun sign brings to that path, your current personal year, the talents you brought with you, and the pain that fuels your work.

1 The birth path that I chose is the vibration of the number
_____.

This means that doing _____work will help me rise to the full potential of what I came here to do.

2 My path is flavored with my sun sign, which is:
This flavor means that my work will have these qualities as part of its mission:

3 Avoiding a tendency to _____ will keep me focused on the highest potential of my path and its expression through my work.

Birth path:

Sun sign:

Personal year:

Talents:

Values:

Pain that fuels me:

CONCLUSION

I have a natural talent for _____,
and I value _____.

My greatest pain fuels me to _____
_____.

Adding those elements to the vibration of my _____ birth path and my
_____ sun sign leads me to consider this type of work: _____.

I will take these three steps to move in the direction of this work:

    1.

    2.

    3.

APPENDIX

A Brief Summary of Scientific Research on
Our Ability to Affect Reality

The power of our thoughts to affect reality has been investigated in the lab by physicists such as William A. Tiller, Ph.D., a former professor at Stanford University and an associate editor of two scientific journals who has published more than two hundred fifty scientific papers in his fifty-two-year-long scientific career. His research, replicated in several controlled laboratory settings across the country, shows that when human beings intentionally concentrate on vials of purified water, their minds can increase the pH of that water by several units—with no chemical additions to the air or water.

According to Tiller, coauthor of *Conscious Acts of Creation: The Emergence of a New Physics*, when individual minds focus their attention on anything, a quantum energy surge occurs, which has a physical and measurable effect on our "reality."

Again and again, in various rigorous scientific experiments (with the results published in major scientific journals, such as *Journal of Scientific Exploration, American Journal of Cardiology,* and *International Journal of Psychophysiology*), Tiller has demonstrated the power of our thoughts.

"There is a consciousness that is a measurable energy, and that consciousness is a core element of life. . . . Our intention changes physical reality," reports Tiller.

Physicist Amit Goswami, Ph.D., in his book *The Self-Aware Universe*, says that we must give up our precious assumption that there is an objective reality out there independent of consciousness. He explains that the universe is "self-aware" and that it is consciousness itself that creates the physical world. He comes to this conclusion by way of quantum physics.

Goswami, currently a senior resident researcher at the Institute of Noetic Sciences, contends that we are creating every moment of "reality" as we go along—with our consciousness. "Naturally we project that the moon is always there in space-time, even when we are not looking. Quantum physics says no. When we are not looking, the moon's possibility wave spreads, albeit by a minuscule amount. When we look, the wave collapses instantly; thus the wave could not be in space-time. . . . There is no object in space-time without a conscious subject looking at it."

In his book, *Physics of the Soul*, Goswami, who taught physics for thirty-two years and was a professor of theoretical science at the University of Oregon, explains this concept in more detail: "Suppose we release an electron in a room. In a matter of moments, the electron wave spreads all over the room. And now suppose we set up a grid of electron detectors, called Geiger counters, in the room. Do all the counters go ticking? No. Only one of the Geiger counters ticks. Conclusion? Before observation, the electron does spread all over the space, but only as a wave of possibility. Observation brings about the collapse of the possibility wave into an actual event."

Dean Radin, Ph.D., Laboratory Director at the Institute of Noetic Sciences and author of *The Conscious Universe* and *Entangled Minds* has spent decades in the lab exploring psychic phenomenon as evidence of our "entanglement" described in quantum physics. His research shows how our thoughts and feelings are accessible to everyone—through the quantum field.

Entanglement, a prediction of quantum theory that Einstein couldn't quite believe (calling it "spooky action at a distance"), refers to connections between separated particles that persist regardless of distance. These connections, says Radin, imply that at very deep levels, the separations that we see between ordinary, isolated objects are illusions created by our limited perceptions. "The bottom line is that physical reality is connected in ways we're just beginning to understand," he explains.

Radin believes that entanglement suggests a scenario that ultimately leads to a vastly improved understanding of psychic phenomena such as telepathy, clairvoyance, and precognition. In his laboratory studies, he has found overwhelming evidence of our human ability to hear each other's thoughts and predict the future. This repeatable laboratory evidence suggests that we have the capacity to perceive distant information and to influence distant events across space and time, he reports.

"Someday psi (psychic phenomena) research will be taught in universities with the same aplomb as today's elementary economics and biology. It will no longer be considered controversial, but just another facet of Nature one learns as part of a well-rounded education," he concludes. "In that future, no one will remember that psi was once considered the far fringe of science."

Bruce Lipton, Ph.D., cell biologist and author of *The Biology of Belief*, has demonstrated in the lab that every gene has a switch that we either turn on or off—with our thoughts, beliefs, and emotions. We are not simply products of our genetic makeup, he concludes; by a subconscious process not yet clearly understood we are choosing which genes to activate and which to ignore. "Genes-as-destiny theorists have obviously ignored hundred-year-old science about enucleated cells, but they cannot ignore new research that undermines their belief in genetic determination," he explains.

While the Human Genome Project was making headlines, a group of scientists were inaugurating a new, revolutionary field in biology called epigenetics. The science of epigenetics (which literally means "control above genetics") profoundly changes our understanding of how life is controlled. In the last decade, epigenetic research has established that DNA blueprints passed down through genes are not set in concrete at birth. "Genes are not destiny!" says Lipton.

Environmental influences, including nutrition, stress, and emotions, can modify those genes, without changing their basic blueprint, he explains. "And those modifications, epigeneticists have discovered, can be passed to future generations as surely as DNA blueprints are passed on."

The character of our lives is determined not by our genes but by our responses to the environmental signals that propel life, he says. "The belief that we are frail biochemical machines controlled by genes is giving way to an understanding that we are powerful creators of our lives and the world in which we live," concludes Lipton, who taught cell biology at the University of Wisconsin's School of Medicine and later performed pioneering studies at Stanford University's School of Medicine.

Candace Pert, Ph.D., internationally recognized pharmacologist and author of *Molecules of Emotion* and *Everything You Need to Know to Feel Go(o)d*, has shown in the lab how our emotions affect our immune systems. Your thoughts and feelings have a direct impact on the behavior of your cells, she reports. Her experiments illustrate that the mind is not focused in the head but distributed throughout molecules in the body. Thus, she says, proper use of the mind can create health in a sick body.

"There is no objective reality," she explains. "In order for the

brain not to be overwhelmed by the constant deluge of sensory input, some sort of filtering system must enable us to pay attention to
what our bodymind deems the most important pieces of information and to ignore the others. Our emotions decide what is worth
paying attention to."

Pert's groundbreaking research also illustrates the addictive nature
of our emotions. When we repeatedly react to our environmental
circumstances by feeling angry, for example, feeling angry becomes
an addictive response to our world that physically changes receptor
sites on certain cells. Eventually those cells require the chemicals pro-
duced by feeling anger on a daily basis in order to survive. Thus we
look for situations that make us angry, so we can get our emotionally
addictive chemical needs met.

Pert contends that we can change this chemical pattern when we
interrupt the cause-and-effect response we have to our environment.
For example, if we choose to laugh instead of yell in a situation that
usually makes us angry, we begin to change our cellular receptor sites.
Eventually those cells become addicted to the feeling of laughter instead of anger, explains Pert. "You can literally become the architect of
your cellular structures—including your immune system—by choosing which emotions to feel consistently on a daily basis."

WHAT TO DO NEXT

Now that you understand what you were put on earth to do, here's a list of recommended books and Web sites to help you on your journey.

Knock 'em Dead Resumes. Martin Yate. Avon, MA: Adams Media Corp., 2008.

Knock 'em Dead Cover Letters. Martin Yate. Avon, MA: Adams Media Corp., 2008.

Knock 'em Dead 2009: The Ultimate Job Search Guide. Martin Yate. Avon, MA: Adams Media Corp., 2008.

How to Land Your Dream Job: No Resume! And Other Secrets to Get You in the Door. Jeffrey J. Fox. New York: Hyperion, 2006.

The Successful Business Plan, 4th Edition: Secrets and Strategies. Rhonda Abrams and Paul Barrow. Palo Alto, CA: The Planning Shop, 2003.

The One Page Business Plan for the Creative Entrepreneur. Jim Horan. Berkeley, CA: The One Page Business Plan Company, 2004.

The One Page Business Plan for Non-Profit Organizations. Jim Horan. Berkeley, CA: The One Page Business Plan Company, 2007.

How to Form a Nonprofit Corporation. 8th ed. Anthony Mancuso. Berkeley, CA: NOLO, 2007.

How to Make It Big as a Consultant. 3rd ed. William A. Cohen. American Management Association, Saranac Lake, NY: AMACOM, 2001.

Small Business Start-Up Kit. 5th ed. Peri Pakroo. Berkeley, CA: NOLO, 2008.

Book Proposals That Worked! Real Book Proposals That Landed $10K–$100K Publishing Contracts. Angela J. Hoy. Splinter Press, 2008.

How to Write a Book Proposal. 3rd ed. Michael Larsen. Cincinnati, OH: Writer's Digest Books, 2004.

Physics of the Soul. Amit Goswami, Ph.D. Charlottesville, VA: Hampton Roads, 2001.

The Holographic Universe. Michael Talbot. New York: Harper Perennial, 1991.

Entangled Minds. Dean Radin, Ph.D. New York: Paraview, 2006.

Molecules of Emotion. Candace Pert, Ph.D. New York: Scribner, 1997.

Some Science Adventures with Real Magic. William A. Tiller, Ph.D. Walnut Creek, CA: Pavior Publishing, 2005.

The Biology of Belief. Bruce Lipton, Ph.D. Mountain of Love / Elite Books, 2005.

Web Sites You Might Find Helpful

http:// online.onetcenter.org
www.payscale.com
www.job-hunt.org
www.monster.com

ABOUT THE AUTHOR

Career intuitive Sue Frederick's work, described as "a breath of fresh air" and "an enlightened new perspective," has been featured in *The New York Times*, *Yoga Journal*, *Natural Health*, and *Fit Yoga* magazines. She's presented workshops at venues such as the Crossings Retreat Center and World Wellness Weekend and for organizations such as the National Hospice Association, the American Business Women's Association, and the National Career Development Association. Her books include *Dancing at Your Desk: A Metaphysical Guide to Job Happiness* and *BrilliantDay: 7 Steps to Turn Your Life Around*. To learn more about her work, visit www .CareerIntuitive.org, e-mail her at sue@brilliantwork.com, or call 303-939-8574.